MANAGING
EMPLOYEE
PERFORMANCE

ISBN: 1-4392-4458-8
EAN13: 9781439244586

Visit www.booksurge.com to order additional copies.

MANAGING EMPLOYEE PERFORMANCE

An Accelerated Learning Text for Supervisors and Students

William F. Hawkins, M.B.A., CM

Table of Contents

Preface

When writing *Managing Employee Performance,* the author selected the best content and accelerated learning activities from hundreds of seminars attended by practicing managers and supervisors in the US, Europe and Asia. While primarily intended as a college level classroom or online text, this practical book is written so that supervisors, managers, team leaders, production leads, and small business owners can learn simply by reading and doing. Jargon is avoided. Understanding how real people learn and improve is emphasized.

Readers will learn to set expectations, analyze and solve performance issues, coach and counsel, and appraise performance. The focus is on the practical application of the knowledge and skills needed by managers and supervisors. College instructors, in-house trainers, managers of supervisors can use it to train people who need to learn and practice the skills. It can serve as a primary or supplemental text. Readings, examples, learning exercises, role plays, and case studies, support an accelerated learning approach.

Special Feature, Support Materials on the Web

Visual aids, games and lectures that supplement *Managing Employee Performance* are available at www.managing-employees.com. Online materials are separate for students and instructors. Many are even fun.

Book Objective

This book provides the building block skills needed to successfully manage the performance of employees on work teams. The ideas and exercises are based on the author's over 30 years of experience developing and training managers and supervisors in North America, Europe and Asia, as well as managing others.

More importantly, every attempt is made to show how the pieces fit together to provide a systematic way to develop high performance. For example, the seventh chapter provides case studies that give the reader an opportunity to integrate the various skills using a directed thinking pattern to analyze performance problems and decide upon corrective actions.

The chapters include text, exhibits, review questions, cases and exercises.

Who Might Benefit from This Book?

➤ College and Post-secondary students as a primary, or supplemental text in a classroom, or online, course
➤ Anyone in a supervisory or coaching role responsible for employee performance management using best practices. This includes **supervisors, managers, team leaders, production leads, and small business owners.**

Student Comments

Here are comments from students who have used the book and materials in class.

➤ I got a lot of value from the assignments. The text is very relevant and easy to understand.
➤ Excellent practical application exercises!!!
➤ Good activities to spark thought process on how one should approach his/her team.
➤ Provided strategies and information I was lacking as a Supervisor. Reflecting, I see my shortcomings and this will fill the gaps in my own performance.
➤ I feel the reading material was simple to read and understand
➤ I liked how much this course relates to everyday work.

A Word about the Job Titles We Use

To simplify the reading, we'll refer to a first level manager (also known as a frontline manager) as a supervisor. The content applies to people holding other job titles such as Owner, Manager, Team Leader, Coach, Foreperson, Project Manager, Project Leader, and other similar jobs. You don't have to have the title "Supervisor" to find the book helpful.

Learning Objectives by Chapter

Chapter 1, Understanding and Illustrating Performance Management Strategy

When you have finished the reading Chapter 1, you will:

- ➤ Identify ways performance management skills benefit you at work and at home
- ➤ Understand the three steps in the supervisory performance management strategy
- ➤ Understand the difference between day-to-day and long-term performance management strategies
- ➤ Understand how performance management activities form a system of communications
- ➤ Differentiate between people-based and information-based performance management system elements
- ➤ Understand how situational factors, such as span, affect the supervisory performance management strategy and needs of the support system
- ➤ Differentiate performance management from the performance appraisal activity
- ➤ List "discriminatory practices" a supervisor should avoid

Chapter 2, Set and Communicate Performance Expectations

When you have completed Chapter 2, you should understand:

- ➤ How to spell out performance expectations
- ➤ How to communicate performance authority and responsibility
- ➤ How to link employee performance expectations to performance and the appraisal

➤ How to set objectives and goals
➤ How to set measurable performance standards
➤ How to set hard-to-measure performance standards
➤ How to keep the big picture in front of employees

Chapter 3, Understanding Two Important People Skills for Solving Performance Problems

When you have finished Chapter 3, you should be able to:
➤ State the difference between descriptive and evaluative feedback
➤ Construct descriptive feedback statements
➤ Offer constructive criticism
➤ Use both direct and non-direct probing styles when analyzing performance shortcomings
➤ Discover the behavioral effects of direct and non-direct probing techniques

Chapter 4, Deciding How to Handle Performance Problems

When you have finished Chapter 4, you will be able to:

➤ State performance problems properly
➤ Apply a performance problem analysis technique
➤ Practice analyzing situations to decide whether to train or to motivate

Chapter 5, The Supervisor as a Trainer

When you have finished Chapter 5, you will be able to:

➤ Consider a developmental style when supervising others
➤ Understand the four stages of job development
➤ Understand the supervisor's role in employee development
➤ Differentiate between strategic and job-level training needs
➤ Choose training strategies that fit the employee's stage of job growth
➤ Determine development responsibilities
➤ Conduct a basic training needs analysis

➤ Identify formal and on-the-job training techniques
➤ Plan to apply basic training techniques such as an orientation plan and a job instruction training plan

Chapter 6, Handling Won't Do Performance Problems: Motivating, Counseling, and Corrective Discipline

When you have finished Chapter 6, you will be able to:

➤ Understand the root of motivational problems
➤ Understand the seven reasons employees appear to lack motivation
➤ Perform a simple behavioral analysis before influencing situations
➤ Practice the steps of the employee counseling interview
➤ Identify the four factors that enhance a disciplined work environment
➤ Understand the steps used when taking disciplinary action with an employee
➤ Identify the components of a performance improvement plan.

Chapter 7, Integrative Case Studies: Putting all the Pieces Together

Integrative Case Studies: Putting all the Pieces Together. This chapter allows practice integrating the earlier chapter material to handle common employee performance challenges. In addition, the reader is encouraged to apply the techniques to their own situation. By doing the elements of this case, the reader should internalize an analysis pattern that integrates performance management concepts, skills, and techniques.

Chapter 8, Performance Appraisals that Support the Day-to-Day Strategy

When you have finished Chapter 8, you will be able to:

➤ Explain how performance appraisal contributes to managing performance
➤ State why good documentation is a prerequisite for accurate ratings
➤ State the three major objectives for performance appraisal discussion

➤ Practice the steps for conducting a performance appraisal discussion
➤ Develop a list of Do's and Don'ts when conducting a performance appraisal discussion.

Appendix, *Supervisory Management: A Brief Review of the Bigger Picture*

When you have finished the Appendix, you should be able:
➤ To define management
➤ To state the two concerns of management
➤ To state the five functions of management
➤ To relate management activities to management functions and processes

Introduction

Management is getting work done through (and with) other people. Supervisors have a constant balancing act: to get the work out while respecting and caring for the people in the work group. If a supervisor can do his or her work without losing sight of either side of this equation, he or she *will* be successful.

In this book, we stress employee performance management. Performance management is getting work done through and with employees by communicating performance expectations, monitoring and analyzing performance, and correcting or adjusting performance.

Before getting started, you might want to read *Supervisory Management: A Brief Review of the Bigger Picture* in the appendix.

Performance management activity fits well with the management process view, and other schools of management. There is a quick review of the management process to provide a big picture context for managing employee performance. Again, you will find it in the Appendix at the end of the book.

Whether your organization has a traditional or a team culture, you likely will find this review to be helpful. If you are new to all of this, it won't take long, so go to the appendix and dig right in. Even if you're experienced, you should find it a speedy review.

When you are ready, Chapter 1 is waiting.

Chapter One

Understanding and Illustrating Performance Management Strategy

Chapter Objectives

When you have finished Chapter 1, you will:

> ➤ Identify ways performance management skills benefit me at work and at home
> ➤ Understand the three steps in the supervisory performance management strategy
> ➤ Understand the difference between day-to-day and long-term performance management strategies
> ➤ Understanding how performance management activities form a system of communications
> ➤ Differentiate between people-based and information-based performance management system elements
> ➤ Understand how situational factors, such as span, affect the supervisory performance management strategy and support system needs
> ➤ Differentiate performance management from the performance appraisal activity
> ➤ List "discriminatory practices" a supervisor should avoid

A Performance Management Strategy: The Strategies We Use

People get something done more effectively when they have a strategy for doing it. Most people develop habits or strategies for doing daily chores. Getting ready for the day might include bathing, dressing, eating, making sure the kids are ready for school, traveling to work, and so on. There are many possibilities for a morning routine, and each of us may do these things differently, but we still get results.

What about shopping and errands? We have strategies for those too. We might set out to buy gas and wash the car, go to the drycleaners or hardware store, then the supermarket, and, if we still have time, reward ourselves at the coffee shop. A strategy is a cluster of decisions about what goals to pursue, what actions to take, and how to use resources to achieve goals. (ICPM, Management Skills III, 2006, 5). Whether we realize it or not, our strategies have three basic components: goals, decisions, and actions.

If we are shopping, our goal may be simple: bring home stuff that we need. But, even a simple goal has many variables, such as: sub-goals (I'm going to buy healthy food and stay within my budget), self-imposed performance standards (I'm going to be out of the grocery store in half an hour), or pre-made decisions (I'll shop at Big Box Foods on 36th Street).

Our actions might include getting ready, finding the checkbook, creating the shopping list, rounding up the dry cleaning, driving to the shopping center, and comparing and selecting items in a store. With repetition, we perfect our system, arriving in time at a predictable and orderly strategy.

This is why change can be stressful: it disrupts the predictability. If we move to a new house or apartment, our old strategy may not work anymore. Why? Because the elements of our shopping errand system changed.

We have to shop in new stores with unfamiliar layouts and deal with different traffic patterns to get there. The length of time it takes to shop—what took half an hour before might take an hour now—and it may make us late for other things. Perhaps we won't be able to find what we want. We'll have to modify our old strategy to fit a new situation.

We develop similar habits at work, engaging in a process called "job crafting" as we make a job our own. Employees use different strategies from each other, some with great results and some with poor. And, like our previous analogy, change can affect our work situations as well.

At home or on the job, we all depend on strategies and systems to get things done.

Strategies for Supervising Others

Imagine you're at work when your manager stops by your desk. You stop what you are doing and he casually announces that next week you will be promoted to Supervisor, with a capital S. Supervisor.

You feel all warm inside. It sounds fun and challenging: *you* will manage other people. Your paychecks will grow substantially.

Five minutes later, when your heart rate has leveled some, you begin to wonder how you will go about supervising other people. Frankly, you have no idea.

Then the terror sets in as you realize that you will be *responsible* for other people's work. To succeed at your job, you will have to get Doug in shipping to send the right parts to the right locations, you have to get Dave in Finish to quit horsing around, and you'll have to get Cindy in Shipping to start talking to Megan, also in Shipping.

On top of that, you're pretty sure that Dave wanted this promotion, and you're pretty sure he'll hold a grudge. Wow!

Fear not. You aren't the first person to be in this position. You can survive, even flourish, with some help and support from your manager and coworkers. Even the angry ones might get over their anger if you take the right approach.

So how do you go about managing other people? Are there strategies or systems that have worked for others?

Of course there are! There are many who have gone before you and they have written thousands of books on management and leadership. You could, if you so desired, spend two lifetimes becoming an expert on the subject; but, who are we kidding; you don't have that kind of time.

The good news is that you can manage very well indeed with a simple, tried-and-true strategy. The beauty of this strategy is that it is widely accepted among employers so you'll be able to take it with you if your next big job is with a different company.

The Three Steps of the Day-To-Day Performance Management Strategy

1. Set work expectations
2. Monitor and analyze actual work against expectations
3. Take corrective action(s)

These three steps are conceptually simple, but can be difficult in practice, requiring skill and maturity to do right. How the steps are practiced is affected by the culture and policies of the employer. The nature of the work being done determines the frequency of the interaction between supervisors and employees. The steps are consistent with behavioral theories and form the basis of people management—the best managers are those who perform these steps consistently, over and over.

The rest of the book, from here on out, is all about setting work expectations, monitoring and analyzing work, and taking corrective actions to handle problems. These actions provide an initiating structure to make sure work is done.

Just as people have strategies for starting their days or doing shopping errands, good managers have strategies for managing employee performance. Flexibility is a must, as is the drive to continuously improve our strategies and interpersonal managerial skills. While the basic steps of good management do not change, our specific strategies need to be adaptable to enable us to cope with changing situations.

How Does Performance Appraisal Fit In?

Every now and then, people stop and take stock of how things are going.

Once they've taken a good look, they make decisions, some big and some small, about how to improve matters. Here are three examples:

1. Sara realizes that her shopping and errand strategy doesn't work as well as it used to. A new highway has disrupted the traffic flow, and the dry cleaner sold out to some incompetent idiot who ruined her favorite suit. It's a small issue, but her time off is limited and clothes don't grow on trees. The time has come to take action—it's time for a new strategy.

2. Mike realizes he's ready to handle greater job responsibilities. He could decide to push for a promotion, change companies, or start a business. This is a bigger, longer term, change.

3. John and Heidi take stock of their marriage, and decide to have children. This very big life strategy change will affect all of their future goals, decisions, and actions.

Once again, what is true in life is true in management. Every now and then, supervisors will evaluate—or appraise—the "big picture" to see how well their strategy is working with the team as a group and with individual employees. Supervisors will review all aspects of an employee's job and grade them on how well they are doing. Usually this is called a performance appraisal or a performance evaluation. Larger organizations make an annual ritual of appraisals.

This practice is usually good, though not always. The appraisals can provide much-needed organizational discipline to keep the management staff "under control." If a supervisor knows that they are going to have to appraise the performance of their employees at some future time, then, they must pay closer attention to what their employees do today. In other words, it helps keep employee performance issues "in front" of supervisors.

In the long term, the efforts of all employees are important, and appraisals can provide a stimulus for supervisors to spend time devising ways to help employees perform better. The appraisal session might be a good time to implement any such plan.

The appraisal process is formal, meaning that it is written down and becomes a part of the employee's permanent record. This formal mechanism gives supervisors some leverage, or influence, to make proper performance matter to employees and lets employees know that there are positive and negative consequences for good and bad behaviors.

The Three Steps in Practice

The three steps discussed earlier comprise the day-to-day supervisory strategy. By following the three steps, you are:

1. informally setting expectations

2. monitoring for problems or performance that varies from expectations

3. working out ways to bring performance up to, or beyond, expectations

In a day-to-day work setting, you are *not* sitting down to write a performance appraisal form, or hold a formal appraisal discussion, or set next year's objectives.

To clarify, study Figures 1.1, 1.2, 1.3, and 1.4, shown below. They will illustrate the steps and some of their typical characteristics. You will notice that the performance appraisal is part of a process that looks like a longer-term version of the day-to-day methodology—the three steps are similar, just viewed over a longer timeline, in most cases one year.

Figure 1.1, below: Day-to-Day Performance Management Steps

	Steps	Typical Characteristics
	1. Set work expectations 2. Monitor and compare 3. Take corrective action(s)	➤ Informal communications ➤ Shorter term decisions ➤ Little or no documentation ➤ Purpose is to adjust performance ➤ Smaller issues and decisions ➤ On-going issues

Figure 1.2, below: Work Planning and Appraisal Process Done Over 12 Months

Steps	Typical Characteristics	
1. Jointly set annual work goals at the beginning of the year 2. Summarize performance peaks and valleys during the year 3. Write and discuss the appraisal at the end of the year and set goals for the next year	➤ Formal communication ➤ Longer term issues (*e.g.,* next 12 months) ➤ Done annually ➤ Documented ➤ Purpose is to judge performance ➤ Bigger issues and decisions ➤ Develop follow-up goals which starts step 1 for next year	

The work planning and appraisal process might make more sense if we view it on a timeline. Imagine this simple illustration. In December, we jointly set annual work goals, throughout the year we do the day-to-day steps, and in December we appraise performance, discuss, and close the loop by setting new goals.

Figure 1.3, below: The Work Planning and Appraisal Process Viewed as a Timeline.

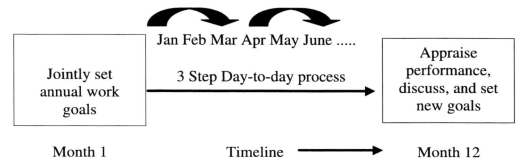

| Jointly set annual work goals | Jan Feb Mar Apr May June .....

3 Step Day-to-day process ——▶ | Appraise performance, discuss, and set new goals |

Month 1   Timeline ——▶   Month 12

As we said, some people and companies might confuse these two processes because they seem so similar. Looking at them side by side in Figure 1.4, we can easily see that the "Annual Work Planning and Appraisal Process" is a big picture, and the other is merely what supervisors do throughout the year to hit the goals. The purposes are different, too.

Figure 1.4, below: Day-to-Day and Appraisal Compared

Day-to-day steps	**Annual Work Planning and Appraisal Process**
1. Set work expectations	1. Jointly set annual work goals at the beginning of the year
2. Monitor and compare	2. Summarize performance peaks and valleys during the year
3. Take corrective action(s)	3. Write and discuss the appraisal at the end of the year and set goals for next year

Another reason people might confuse these is that not all supervisors or leaders do both. Many do the day-to-day and leave appraisal to higher managers. This is not unusual for many supervisors and "leads." You still need to know how to manage performance. You just do not have to do the performance appraisal activity.

All this theory may seem a bit much but, in practice, you will intuitively know the difference between what fits day-to-day and what you should do in the work planning and appraisal process.

Just remember: performance appraisal is periodic, usually a once-a-year activity, and day-to-day performance management steps are an ongoing series of actions that will become second nature to you in your career as a supervisor. If this all were a picture puzzle, the day-to-day steps create and assemble the pieces; and the performance appraisal evaluates the finished picture.

Factors Affecting Strategy

As we discussed at the beginning of the chapter, the strategies a supervisor may employ are a mixture of goals, decisions, and actions and can be fluid depending on the situation.

Following are some factors that can play a role in shaping strategy:

- ➤ Nature of the work or industry
- ➤ Time horizons
- ➤ Work technologies
- ➤ Management styles
- ➤ Span or the headcount of employees directly supervised
- ➤ Organization's culture and values
- ➤ Skills and motivation of the employee(s)
- ➤ Labor relations and union contracts
- ➤ Government regulations
- ➤ Legal environment and constraints
- ➤ Business climate and company's financial position
- ➤ Labor market conditions

The nature of the work—or the nature of the industry—will naturally lead supervisors to select actions that fit the situation. The supervisor of a research engineering team at a semi-conductor company will have a different management strategy than a supervisor of retail clerks at a mall clothing store. Why? The nature of the work tasks and the industries are different.

Another key difference influencing strategy would be the time horizons of projects employees are working on. A time horizon is nothing more than the length of time from when an employee starts a task to when that task is complete. A team of researchers seeking to make a breakthrough in semiconductors may work years before seeing the fruits of their labor. The time it would take to determine sales results in the clothing store would be much shorter. Thus, the researchers have a longer time horizon in their work, and the clothing store employees have a relatively short one.

So, if you quit your job as an engineering supervisor and take a job at the mall, you can expect to manage differently.

Work technologies are another important factor in determining management strategies. The medical staff in the Trauma Unit of a hospital is made up of highly trained professionals working in high stress situations with expensive, customized technology. In another scenario, low-tech production line workers use a chain-linked product technology to perform highly repetitive tasks. Your performance management strategies would differ significantly in both scenarios.

Does the company you're working for favor a team style of management or a command-control style? (What is command-control? Think Army and you'll be in the ballpark.) If your employer does favor a command-control style, you'll be expected to use a tight performance management strategy. If a team style, you'll be influenced toward a more participative strategy. (Think teamwork.)

Are you managing at a union shop or a non-union shop? You can bet the wages, hours, and work rules will vary from one to the other.

Perhaps you're managing workers at an oil refinery—you can expect heavy government regulation, mainly in the form of exhaustively-detailed safety procedures governing employee management.

Most employers today must comply with state and federal government regulations. Here is a representative list of laws, acts, and governing bodies: Equal Employment Opportunity/Affirmative Action, OSHA, and the Americans with Disabilities Act, the Health Department, and the Equal Pay Act.

As you can see, a huge variety of factors influence performance management strategy. If you leave one company for another—even if they are in the same industry and use the same technologies—you may have to adapt your performance management strategy. This could even happen when changing management jobs within the same company.

When you choose a performance management strategy, learn from those who have gone before, expect to be flexible, and do remember the three steps in Figure 1.1.

Systematic Communications

If you take a step back to look at it, the day-to-day activities involved in managing performance fall into a sort of system for communications. Actually, there are a couple of different ways to define what it is that makes a system:

1. A system is a group of interacting, interrelated, or interdependent elements forming a complex whole.

2. A system is a network of structures and channels, as for communication, travel, or distribution.

Structural Communication Elements

The first definition, a group of interrelated elements forming a complex whole, is the one that applies most directly to communications between a supervisor and an employee. In practice, managers choose system elements to support their strategies—remember that the performance management strategy has three steps:

1. Set work expectations

2. Monitor and analyze actual work against expectations

3. Take corrective action(s)

Each of the three steps will have a system element to support it and move the strategy forward. Suppose Maria, mother of 10-year-old Darren, thinks that it is time for him to show more responsibility and to clean up his room—she might implement a system with these three structural elements:

1. Meeting to explain the day's plan (supports setting expectations)

    "Darren, today we are going to clean the house. You're a big kid and I think it's time for you to clean your own room. From now on you will get to clean your own room, just like you have seen me do it. When you clean, make sure you get all your clothes off the floor, and vacuum the carpet. When your room is straightened up, the clothes are put away, and the carpet is vacuumed, then you'll be done."

2. Mid-point inspection tour (Supports monitoring and analyzing work against expectations)

    Maria notices that Darren took everything off the floor in his room . . . and stuffed it in the closet. The clothes are, in fact, off the floor, but the closet door won't shut. Maria steps on a clump of grass and dried-out leaves—apparently, Darren hasn't vacuumed.

3. Coaching session with Darren (Supports to take corrective action)

    "Darren, I see you are making progress—I never imagined that so much could fit in one closet! But, you still need to vacuum, and when you're done with that, please put these dirty clothes in the hamper and hang up the clothes you haven't worn. Then you can go back to your video game, or we could maybe do something together, maybe a movie."

Here is a table showing the structural elements of Maria's system for communicating new responsibilities to Darren.

Basic Strategy	System Structural Element
Set expectations	Meeting to explain the day's plan
Monitor and analyze actual work against expectations	Mid-point inspection tour
Take corrective action	Coaching session

In order to be sure that Darren gets the work done, all three steps have to happen in order. It wouldn't work well to just have the initial meeting and leave the results to chance—Darren wouldn't learn. And even if Maria got lucky and Darren did a superb job the first time, she has no indication that he will do a good job the next time around unless she talks to him. When she coaches him, she is passing on a skill and, at the same time, recognizing his effort and thus motivating him.

Her system requires all three structural elements: the meeting, the tour, and coaching to support the basic strategy. It structures her *performance management communications system.*

System as Network

The parts or structural elements of Maria's system are simple, people-based, and documented only in her mind. In companies today, there are very sophisticated system tools available to management. According to the second definition mentioned earlier, *a system is a network of structures and channels, as for communication, travel, or distribution.*

The second definition applies mostly to the organizational system elements supervisors and employees use to ensure that the work is done. These systems are often simple, effective, and paper-based. They provide a more complex initiating structure for work.

They can range from simple restroom cleaning checklists at the airport to traditional patient charts and medication records in a hospital. Placing colored stickers on a coffee-stained notebook page at a garage, or yard, sale becomes a simple "inventory control" system.

Businesses use a number of management information systems (MIS) to provide these elements. The systems can vary dramatically depending on the industry or the department within a company. They can be as simple as a daily checklist and as complex as a vast network of conveyor belts and scanners with information routed to server accessed by hundreds or thousands of computers.

Almost any business operating today needs some level of information management network: manufacturers, retailers, airlines, healthcare institutions, process industries, and farmers all use them. Different departments within any given company will have their own systems: sales, order entry, accounts payable and receivable, inventory control, traffic routing, billing, human resources, and payroll all have a need to keep track of large amounts of information.

Of course, the technology employed has changed dramatically: what was once done with pencil and paper is now done with bar codes, punch cards, RF chips, global positioning equipment, and laser readers that feed the data bases that yield the management control information supervisors require.

Supervisors use this abundance of information to determine if the organization's performance is on track by searching and extracting information from various system reports. They use other communication mechanisms to get the information in front of employees who require the information to do their work. Information is a resource that supervisors use, distribute, assign, or share to communicate their expectations and monitor work progress. Figure 1.5 shows examples of people-based and information-based system elements.

People-Based (Employee-Supervisor) System Elements	Information System-Based Source Elements
Setting Expectation Activities ➤ Goal setting meetings ➤ Development planning meetings ➤ Quality Team meetings ➤ Staff meetings ➤ Orienting new hires ➤ Coaching sessions ➤ Discussing decision-making authority ➤ Reviewing job descriptions ➤ Follow-up meetings ➤ Input from experts ➤ Analysts ➤ Industrial Engineers Monitoring Activities ➤ Direct observation ➤ Inspections ➤ Reviewing reports ➤ Status meetings ➤ Project review meetings Correcting Activities ➤ Interpersonal feedback ➤ Criticism ➤ Leading ➤ Motivating ➤ Coaching ➤ Job-instruction training ➤ Disciplinary sessions ➤ Reassignment ➤ Fines	Setting Work Expectations and Monitoring ➤ Budgetary controls ➤ Financial controls ➤ Balance sheets ➤ Income statements ➤ Cash flow ➤ Cost of goods sold ➤ Audits ➤ Project management software ➤ Quality reports ➤ Safety reports ➤ Payroll reports ➤ Inventory reports ➤ Material Requirements Planning (MRP) systems ➤ Master Production Schedule ➤ Bill of materials ➤ Inventory ➤ Enterprise Resource Planning (ERP)

Figure 1.5: People-Based and Information System-Based Elements

To be effective, supervisors need systems that they can trust will work. These systems replace the old coordination meetings, save on shoe leather, and decrease games of phone tag. A good system can put the routine stuff on autopilot and allow time for the critical few exceptions. The elements of a good system should be simple, easy, and flexible.

Words of Caution

Systems need to be current to give a competitive edge in quality and cost. This includes MIS (management information system) support systems as well as production systems that give feedback to employees and supervisors.

In addition, the system serves you and the employee team, not the other way around. Do not let "the system" isolate you from the flesh and blood people on your team. People work for you, not the system.

Overall, there is still no substitute for good, old-fashioned, face time.

Span, Team Size and Your Time

Span is the number of people reporting to a supervisor. If you have a few people, you have a narrow span. If you have many people, we call it a broad span. Few and many are relative terms when talking about span, and there are different considerations when deciding the "right" number. For example, new supervisors likely do better with a narrow span (few people) while learning supervisory job basics.

If you only have a few people on your team, five for example, you should have time to perform the people-based and information-based activities shown in Figure 1.5. If you have a broad span, forty-five for example, you will have less per-person time to do all of these activities. This would be especially true if the five and the forty-five all have the same job description.

Here we are trying to make only one simple point. *All job factors being equal, the broader the span, the more critical it is that you have a good performance management system in place.* Without it, the numerous people-based performance management activities in Figure 1.5, such as directly observing work, consume too much time to be realistic.

Organizations today have *flatter structures*. In other words, they have fewer levels of management between the workers and the top person. There are many reasons for a flat structure including lower management overhead costs and other productivity benefits. Another reason is computer technology makes it now possible. This trend affects the supervisor because flat organizations tend to have broad spans.

If you have a very broad span, you will need information system-based tools such as a MRP[i] or an Enterprise Resource Planning, ERP, system. If these aren't in place, create do-it-yourself tools such as workflow sheets, checklists, or daily production control visuals of some type. Even a whiteboard and colored markers might be useful tools.

Bottom line: the bigger the span, the more critical it is that the supervisor has an efficient monitoring system. Daily reports and midday reports are among the tools that can be utilized to show work status and performance shortcomings. Tools and reports direct the supervisor's time and attention to the most critical problems and opportunities.

Skills of a Good Supervisor

Performance management activities mostly fall under the functions of planning, controlling and evaluating.[ii] However, in order to translate all the good thinking into action, supervisors need certain competencies or skills.

Perhaps this is a reason start up business owners develop headaches after their business grows; and they have to hire employees to handle the abundance of customers. Let us consider master auto mechanic, Brett.

Brett started out repairing cars in his home garage. Soon business backed up, he had customers clamoring for service, and his wife was complaining about gasoline smells and vehicles leaking oil all over the driveway. Brett took his customer list, his strong technical skills, a little saved capital, and rented the old service station with three service bays that closed soon after the Route 28 bypass went through. Not good for gas sales, but all agreed that it was a great location for Brett's Master Auto Repair.

He hired three employees: an old tech school buddy, one off his "Help Wanted" sign, and the self-proclaimed expert mechanic he met Friday night at Stewee's Pub. That's when Brett's headaches started. He had the strong technical skills for auto repair, but now he spent much of the day facing challenges of a different sort. He also needs competencies of a different sort. Without intent, Brett became a supervisor.

Brett thought that managing employee performance was just common sense and he usually has plenty of that. While it's certainly true that you'd have a hard time being an effective supervisor without common sense, common sense alone won't do the job. To be effective a supervisor must have three basic skill sets: people skills, thinking skills, and technical skills.

Supervisors need thinking skills to do the intellectual heavy lifting of planning, organizing, controlling, and evaluating. Though valuable, none of that thought will be worth much if a supervisor cannot communicate their great concepts and ideas to the team. To judge whether the work is correct, a supervisor has to have knowledge or skill in the technical work the team members do. So, thinking skills for the big picture, people communication skills to give the effort legs, and technical skills to check that the work is right—all three are essential for good supervision. Brett has to learn new skills quickly or risk losing his good reputation.

People skills, especially communication, deserve underscoring. One could have exceptional thinking skills and exceptional technical skills and still be a poor supervisor. People skills translate the value of the other two skill sets into action. That's why our following chapters will emphasize performance management communication techniques used to influence others to perform. Brett confides he could use them now with all three of his new employees, especially the "expert" he hired last Friday at Stewee's Pub.

The Legal Environment

Understanding the legal matters surrounding employees and their rights is a great example of a key thinking skill. It is imperative that a supervisor have a functional understanding of Federal and State laws governing employment. Legal matters are conceptual by their very nature and require supervisors to have the ability to operate within the policy and authority limits provided by their employers. Supervisors have a legal responsibility to perform within the framework of the laws offering legal protection to employees.

The following is a brief list of the federal laws prohibiting job discrimination:

➤ Title VII of the Civil Rights Act of 1964 prohibits employment discrimination based on race, color, religion, sex, or national origin.
➤ The Equal Pay Act of 1963 (EPA) protects men and women who perform substantially equal work in the same establishment from sex-based wage discrimination.
➤ The Age Discrimination in Employment Act of 1967 (ADEA) protects individuals who are 40 years of age or older.
➤ Title I of the Americans with Disabilities Act of 1990 (ADA) prohibits employment discrimination against qualified individuals with disabilities who work in the federal government.

➤ Section 501 of the Rehabilitation Act of 1973 prohibits discrimination against qualified individuals with disabilities who work in the federal government.
➤ The Civil Rights Act of 1991 provides monetary damages in cases of intentional employment discrimination.
➤ The Equal Employment Opportunity Commission (EEOC) enforces all of these laws. EEOC also provides oversight and coordination of all federal equal employment opportunity regulations, practices, and policies.

You can learn more information and keep up to date about U. S. Federal laws at http://www.eeoc.gov.

Review Questions

Please answer the following questions as a review.

1. What are the steps in the day-to-day performance management strategy?

2. What effects does change have on our performance management strategies?

3. How does yearly performance appraisal provide a structure for a company's performance management efforts?

4. A Supervisor says, "I see no reason to change the way I've been supervising over the years." What might be wrong with this thinking?

5. If a supervisor's span increases dramatically, what could help them manage the performance of the larger number of employees?

6. What role does each of the three basic skill sets play in successful supervisory performance management?

7. What is a strategy?

8. Name at least two factors that could affect one's performance management strategy. Explain how each might affect the strategy.

9. Team leader, Pat, starts each day with a 10 minute meeting to outline the employee quality improvement tasks that day. Pat checks with the employees throughout the day to problem solve and coach. We might consider the meeting, the checking, the coaching and problem solving all to be structural elements of Pat's performance management _____ system. (Please fill in the blank.)

10. In the United States, what federal agency provides oversight and coordination of all federal equal employment opportunity regulations, practices, and policies?

Chapter One Learning Activities

1. Introduction: Remember the case of Maria and her son, Darren. Maria had her structural elements that supported the three basic steps of the performance management strategy which are 1) set expectations, 2) monitor and compare, and 3) correct.

Learning activity: What are the structural elements of a (the) performance management system for your job or for your class?

    1.   1a. What are the effects of the elements on performance?

2. Introduction: Please recall Figure 1.3 below, which shows the structural elements (parts) of a performance appraisal system. Notice the first element, jointly set annual work goals; and the last element, appraise performance are communication activities.

Figure 1.3,

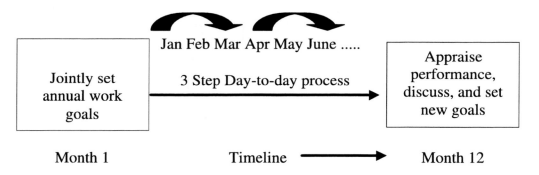

Learning activity: Please list similar communication activities from Figure 1.5 for the middle element, the *3-Step Day-to-day process*, by writing them in the proper category below:

    2a. Set work expectations

    2b. Monitor and analyze actual work against expectations

    2c. Take corrective action(s)

3. Write 1-3 paragraphs on the topic:

As I see it today, learning to "Managing Performance" can benefit me in my work and/or my family life in the following ways:

4. Internet Exercise
Go to http://www.eeoc.gov. Browse the site to identify and list at least three "discriminatory practices" a supervisor should avoid.

Chapter Two
Set and Communicate Performance Expectations

Chapter Objectives

When you have finished the reading, you should understand:

- ➤ How to spell out performance expectations
- ➤ How to communicate performance authority and responsibility
- ➤ How to link employee performance expectations to performance and the appraisal
- ➤ How to set objectives and goals
- ➤ How to set measurable performance standards
- ➤ How to set hard-to-measure performance standards
- ➤ How to keep the big picture in front of employees

As we discussed in the last chapter, the day-to-day steps have three parts: setting work expectations, monitoring results and comparing them against plan, and taking corrective actions. Having a meeting of the minds about performance expectations is the starting point.

The Value of Setting Expectations for Performance Management

All behavior is goal directed. Supervisors want employee behaviors to be directed toward their work expectations and not something else. Later on, we address some tricky aspects of goals and motivation, but for now, we will assume that work goals motivate performance. By the way, some people get hung up whether the words "goal" and "objective" have different meanings. While they might in certain organization settings, here they do not. Here they both mean a hoped for result or outcome.

If supervisors want to see results, and they do, then obviously they will want to communicate what they expect to see. Before getting into the details, let's understand what we hope to accomplish when we set expectations:

- ➤ To set goals to stimulate performance behavior
- ➤ To clarify performance targets to enhance motivation
- ➤ To provide performance "checkpoints" or markers
- ➤ To reduce interpersonal and team member conflict
- ➤ To improve team coordination
- ➤ To provide an objective basis for evaluating employees

The rest of this chapter identifies different kinds of work expectations and how to set them.

What's the Mission?

Setting work expectations begins with helping an employee understand his or her job's purpose or mission. You might use a mission statement to do this: "Harry, it is imperative that we maintain our reputation for innovation. I'd like you to think of your job in those terms." Another example of a mission statement might be "Quality is job one," or "Customer service is our most important product."

Giving an employee a sense of their job's purpose can help them understand how they fit in and help them take pride in their work.

Structuring Job Responsibilities

For employees to be productive team members, they must know their responsibilities. This is a fundamental part of supervisory delegation. In addition, there are few things more frustrating to employees than struggling to meet unclear responsibilities only to find out that they did the wrong thing.

For maximum clarity, a good supervisor will sit down with an employee to outline clear responsibilities and priorities for their job. Maria works on a toy assembly line, and her responsibilities include the following:

> ➤ Prepare for shift by ensuring her station has adequate supplies
> ➤ Snap four wheels onto each passing remote control car
> ➤ Check wheels for proper fit
> ➤ Insert circuit modules
> ➤ Clean up area when shift is over
> ➤ Participate on the quality team

Aside from quality team participation, Maria's job responsibilities are very clear. Before her shift, she must ensure that her station is adequately supplied. For each car that comes by, she must put on the wheels, check them for fit, and insert the circuit module. Then, when her shift is over, she must clean her station.

Prioritizing Job Responsibilities

Sherry is an engineer working on a team designing a new and improved garbage truck. Her job responsibilities will not be quite as cut and dry as Maria's. Sherry's responsibilities include:

➤ Design the hydraulic arms that lift the truck bed
➤ Design the claw that picks up the garbage cans and dumps them
➤ Coordinate with other team members to ensure proper ergonomics for the sanitation workers
➤ Serve as group point person
➤ Communicate periodically with the truck builder

Maria's job has clear responsibilities with very short time horizons. Sherry's job also has clear responsibilities, but Sherry has some flexibility in how she accomplishes her tasks and has a longer time horizon for her project. She must learn to prioritize her responsibilities and use her time well in order to meet her goals.

Who's the Decision Maker?

Decades ago, a command-control management style dominated American industry. Under this system, most significant decisions were made by a title-holder (i.e. supervisor, manager, president, CEO, etc.) and the decision making processes were very centralized. Companies had a hard and fast distinction between management—the "thinkers"—and employees, or "doers."

Employers now empower employees to make decisions to a greater degree than ever before. People with the relevant information and expertise who are closest to the action make faster decisions. This eliminates bureaucracy, lowers costs, and makes performance nimble. This is certainly the case for Sherry's job; and more productions jobs like Maria's are organized using empowered teams.

For now, Maria makes few decisions —her responsibilities are clear, and the work situation will change little from day to day. Sherry's job, on the other hand, will require her to make multiple decisions daily. It would be unduly restrictive if she had to check with her supervisor every time she had a decision to make or a question to handle.

Her supervisor will have to spell out for Sherry what sorts of decisions she can make on her own, what sorts of decisions she will need to make in collaboration with a team, and what sorts of decisions she will have to discuss with her supervisor. Her authority will expand too as she can handle it.

Whether an employee has a job like Maria's or one like Sherry's, they need to know the boundaries of their decision making authority.

Work Expectations Affect Motivation

Usually, the formal performance appraisal is conducted once a year. Because of their infrequency, performance appraisals do not have much short-term motivational value. Psychologists tell us that goals that are more than 30 days out have limited motivational value. Therefore, it is the day-to-day standards that do the real heavy lifting when it comes to employee motivation.

Consider an American football team: ultimately, they're trying to get to the goal line to score a touchdown. You could say that reaching the end zone is their goal every time they have possession of the ball. The team can track their progress toward the goal by the yard markers on the field and they have a number of smaller, more easily attainable goals along the way— first downs.

Take Sherry's task of designing a garbage truck. Let's say her team's end goal for the project is 12 months. If Sherry's supervisor is wise, he or she will break that project down into weekly or monthly bites, creating 12 (or more) deadlines to hit instead of just a big one at the end. This helps motivate Sherry on an ongoing basis during the project.

Work expectations are the standards of performance that apply to the employee's work every day. They have motivational value in that they let the employee know when they have succeeded and how well they are progressing. Work expectations form the baseline of the annual performance appraisal.

What's my Objective?

Some may recall the *Mission Impossible* movies when Secret Agent Ethan Hunt gets his self-destructing job assignment. They always refer to it as his "objective" as in: "Ethan, your objective is to ferret out a mole in our European Headquarters."

An objective is like a mission: what does the company need an employee or team of employees to accomplish? As supervisors, how do we know if we are providing our employees with well-stated work objectives? For starters, we can look at three criteria:

> Would a reasonably qualified person think the expectations are clear?
> Are the objectives measurable?
> Is there an accountability mechanism built in?

Objectives that are clear, measurable, and accountable will have great motivational value for employees.

The Clarity Test

An objective statement should be complete and clear, and contain the following elements:

> An action
> An expected result
> A time span or time frame
> A statement of people and other resources

Let's look at an example for Sherry's garbage-truck-designing team: "To complete a full, workable design of a new garbage collection truck by September 15th. The truck will have 25% more capacity than the previous model, 15% greater fuel efficiency, and improved ergonomics for the sanitation workers to aid in preventing repetitive motion injuries. We will use four engineers and materials at a cost of $190,000."

Do you see all the elements of a good objective statement in the example? The action is completing a new garbage truck. The time frame is "by September 15th." The expected result is a truck with 25% more capacity, 15% greater fuel efficiency and improved ergonomics. The statement of people and resources is the four engineers and materials at a cost of $190,000.

Standards for Measurability and Accountability

Standards further help to define objectives and give them life and meaning on a day-to-day basis. For cyclical, routine, and repetitive tasks like Maria's job assembling remote control cars and their control units, her job objective is the standard itself: do the cars have all four wheels properly attached as they pass her station? Do the circuit boards have the two components in place?

For longer terms—project or developmental objectives, like the truck Sherry's team is designing—the standards further define the objectives. The standards complete the statement: "Performance is up to expectation when . . ."

Typically, standards are quantifiable, expressed numerically, and are easy-to-measure. They answer some or all of the questions in the following list:

➤ How much?
➤ By when?
➤ In what manner?
➤ At what cost?
➤ With what accuracy/precision/quality?

Numerical standards for an installer might look like this: "To install 50 units per month, in accordance with best practice work methods for safety, at a cost of $150 per unit, with fewer than one callback per twenty installs."

A supervisor does not have to address *all* of these questions each time they communicate standards to an employee, they just have to be sure to address the *right* questions when they sit down for a meeting of the minds.

A bank Teller's (Clerk's) numerical standard might be expressed as a ratio or percentage: to serve 15 customers per hour during peak periods. *This sort of standard is meaningful when the supervisor is comparing actual performance to a reference point that is accepted or desired.* This standard may be compared to other Tellers at the bank, the best Teller currently at the bank, or the best Teller the manager has ever known.

Key indicators are another type of numerical standard that is useful in certain situations. An example of a key indicator might be the number of complaints about rude treatment filed against customer service personnel. *Key indicators are only useful as "indirect measures."* If a customer service supervisor is present with an employee, the employee is likely to be pleasant to customers, but if the supervisor is absent, the employee may be rude.

Ranges and "Performance is up to Expectation When . . ."

As we stated earlier, all expectations and standards really complete the statement: "Performance is up to expectation when …"

While that phrase provides us with an effective way to talk about performance, we must be careful in framing the discussion. Many employees, upon hearing "performance is up to expectation when you complete 50 units per hour," may feel that 50 units is their goal for the day. Though they may be capable of more than 50 units per hour, they might feel that it's unnecessary and do fewer. Of course part of a supervisor's job is to encourage people to work up to their potential, so we should avoid expressing standards of performance in terms of fixed points—such as 50 units—but rather use ranges of performance.

People get a better idea of what is expected when a supervisor communicates the standard as a range or scale of performance. Take speed of routine service, for example. A supervisor could communicate to an employee that, if you're serving three customers per hour, that's poor performance. However, if you're serving seven customers per hour, that's pretty good performance. And if I see you serving ten or more customers per hour, I'm going to think that's excellent performance.

If a range isn't possible, try to communicate some point of comparison. For example, if part of person's job is to secure certain files, the points of comparison might be: "Locked files are secure, and unlocked files are not secure." This is clearer than the open-ended directive "Secure the files." This brings up the topic of result descriptions and checklists as standards.

Result Descriptions

Earlier in the chapter, we discussed Sherry's team designing a better garbage truck. They have a long job ahead of them and so their supervisor has decided to implement milestone performance indicators as result descriptions. By setting 12 benchmark goals, one goal for each month that Sherry's team will be working on the project, the supervisor will be able to keep closer tabs on the project as it progresses.

To execute the plan Sherry's team might decide to work with the supervisor to come up with a chart that links major milestone results to the calendar dates. Milestone results can be checked off on the chart when completed.

Checklists can be useful in a wide variety of settings. Supervisors who are not present for all shifts may have employees fill out a checklist at the end of a shift. It might be just a list of key tasks that could be done each shift with a place for "yes" or "no" checkmarks. For example, a night shift employee completes it, and the day supervisor monitors and verifies results.

Hospitals, nursing homes, and other facilities that administer medications require employees to sign off on medications after they are given. Salespeople often have sales tracks, which are benchmarks along the way to closing a sale. These are all result descriptions.

A list of task steps can be a result description. To illustrate, let's use a bank Teller as an example. Here is a result description that shows the steps used to train a new bank Teller to cash a check for a customer

1. Get customer in line

2. Begin transaction

3. Receive check

4. Get endorsement

5. Inspect check

6. Count out cash

7. Thank customer

The seven steps in this result description guide the new Teller all the way through the transaction, from the time the customer first steps in line to thanking them for their business. In a very short time, the Teller will, not only have a mental map for cashing a customer check, but also, they will associate customer service actions with each step.

For example, after thanking the departing customer, the Teller might turn and establish eye contact with the next customer in line. As they receive the check, they may have a service tip to smile at the customer. When receiving the endorsement, they may want to establish eye contact again. They will go on like this until they thank the customer for their business and look to the next customer, thus starting the steps over.

General Descriptions

General descriptions are another good tool to clarify hard-to-measure work expectations. They operate on the "picture is worth a thousand words" concept. For instance, a supervisor might utilize an A/B comparison with two reports, one being very neat and one being sloppy. Seeing a tangible example will help the employee understand what is expected in future reports. The supervisor can point out positive aspects of the neat report and discuss flaws in the sloppy report.

A supervisor orienting new janitorial staff might discuss the merits of clean versus dirty bathrooms, giving the new staff specific items to watch for. A graphic artist's supervisor might show examples of clean and cluttered page layouts.

For customer service people moving in and out of customer's homes—carpenters, plumbers, movers, and the like—a supervisor may use representative before and after photos of the service site to show what their expectations are for site appearance before leaving.

The beauty of general descriptions as well as result descriptions is that, once supervisors come up with them, they can be used repeatedly for new hires, and people moving in and out of the work unit.

Behavioral Descriptions

Supervisors all over the world would like their employees to be motivated, work well together, show initiative, and be problem-solvers. However, what do these things really mean? An action that is seen as bold and showing initiative in one company might be seen as overstepping bounds in another.

Since these universally desired attributes may look different in different settings, how does a supervisor describe them properly? They do so with behavioral descriptions. A behavioral description simply describes something an employee says or does (or doesn't do) and not the supervisor's opinion of it. Thus, the description stays in the realm of the observable behavior and stays away from giving unsolicited opinions on those actions.

Later we will see that the ability to describe behavior is critical when giving feedback, coaching or counseling an employee, or setting expectations. Good supervisors are unconsciously competent at behavioral descriptions.

Though the technique for setting behavioral descriptions seems simple, most people find it to be a bit tricky. How do we come up with behavioral descriptions? Here is a common sense suggestion. Think about a person who is a good example of the behaviors that you hope to see. (This could be you.) Decide what the specific behaviors are that earn your high opinion. Try to be specific about the things they say and do. Communicate and stress those same behaviors with your employees. Let's think about some examples.

Suppose you ask a new employee to take initiative. The employee would have every right to ask, "What does initiative mean around here?" and expect a reasonable answer. (Who knows, maybe they got into trouble at their old job by showing initiative!) You can go on to clarify performance behaviors: "If you see a problem with a customer, I expect you to immediately help them solve that problem, or for example, to start a project without being asked to do so. If I see you doing those kinds of things, I'll know you're showing some initiative." The behaviors described add examples of what "initiative," means on your team.

Similarly, a supervisor might tell team members, "I want you all to cooperate. What I mean by that is I'd like to see you help each other out, cross-train one other, give each other tips, offer help and so on." Again, the behaviors described add clear examples of what you mean by "cooperate."

Developing this skill may take a little discipline. The payoff is employees get a clear idea of how to conduct themselves.

Thinking Ahead to the Performance Appraisal When Setting Expectations

When setting expectations, think ahead to when you have to fill out the performance appraisal form. It is easy to get immersed in details and miss communicating a few critical categories of performance that are easy for everyone to remember. In addition, it is only fair that we give advanced notice of how we will judge overall performance at appraisal time. When communicating work expectations, it is good practice to let people know what those overall factors are and will be. In other words, after discussing all the details, it is a good idea to step back and communicate a few "main mission" categories.

When these are in place, you have a shorthand way to reinforce the "Big Picture" or "The Critical Few" performance factors. These will vary from one job to another.

Before looking at a suggestion about how this might work, we note that many performance appraisal forms require a manager to rate an employee on a range or scale from unsatisfactory to excellent performance. If you as a supervisor don't have a clear idea of your overall rating criteria, when the appraisal rolls around your ratings may appear to be capricious and subjective.

Communicating the Critical Few

Here is a suggestion. Consider summarizing all the work expectations into three catchall categories that cover most of them. They are the *work results, teamwork, and development*. Furthermore, let's say that these are equally important to your overall performance opinion of all employees. Let's clarify first what these are, and then look at how they might help us communicate how we will do our evaluations in the future.

Work results are what first pops into mind regarding employee ratings, because they are the items that face us every hour. It is the work that we quickly hear about when something goes wrong. Examples are, orders filled, jobs shipped, patients served, customers served, reports filed, projects completed, and so on. In other words, what we get paid to accomplish at work. If one asks most managers how they would rate a person on the appraisal, the manager would say, "By evaluating their results." However, when they think about it further, there is more to the evaluation.

Helping other employees or *Teamwork* is also important to the overall rating. We want individual employees to work with others so that the entire team's performance is high. Unless an employee can perform their job in a closet, without interaction with others, teamwork is important. A supervisor's own performance rating depends on how well the entire work team performs, not just on how well any single employee performs. Most of the time, it makes sense for teamwork to be part of the employee rating.

If your company cares about continuous improvement and competitive advantage then you are concerned with *employee development*. In other words, are employees developing in ways that will make us better tomorrow than we are today? Quality, efficiency, responsiveness to customers, and innovation are competitive advantage building blocks that require employees to get better in their jobs.

Skill development and learning are important especially when rating a relatively new employee. Let's consider an enthusiastic, bright, new graduate engineer in a civil engineering firm. If the manager based their rating just on work results, the new engineer's results would likely be poor when compared to a highly experienced engineer. It would be demoralizing and wrong to rate the newcomer as a poor performer, when they are learning as expected or developing quickly. In this situation, the new engineer's overall performance rating gets a boost from their good development progress despite the lower results.

There is a lesson in this too for the experienced engineer, who gets good results today, but can't be bothered to develop their skills to meet changing conditions. Their appraisal rating could drop if they ignore development expectations.

If we now have an idea of what we mean by *results, teamwork*, and *development*, let's look at an example of how they might work when communicating overall work expectations. Consider the following as a range of overall performance from unsatisfactory to top performance. It looks like the part of many performance appraisal forms where one gives an overall rating. Assume you give results, teamwork and development each equal weight of 1/3 in your performance rating, as shown in Figure 2.1.

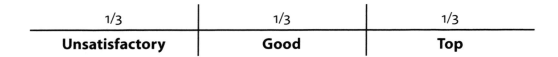

1/3 Results
1/3 Teamwork or helps others
1/3 Development

Figure 2.1

Let's consider Jim. If Jim gets perfect scores in *results*, but does not develop himself nor get any points for teamwork, then he earns the full 1/3 for results and nothing else. Your opinion and Jim's rating might look something like this in Figure 2.2:

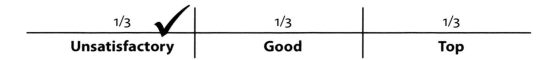

Figure 2.2

If Jim gets perfect scores in *results* and in *teamwork* but does not develop, then he has earned the 1/3 for results and 1/3 for teamwork. He gets no points for development. Your opinion and Jim's rating might look something like this in Figure 2.3:

1/3	1/3 ✔	1/3
Unsatisfactory	**Good**	**Top**

Figure 2.3

If Jim gets perfect scores in *results, teamwork,* and *development,* your opinion and Jim's rating might look something like this superior performance rating in Figure 2.4:

1/3	1/3	1/3 ✔
Unsatisfactory	**Good**	**Top**

Figure 2.4

Of course, if Jim gets average ratings in all three criteria, his rating might look like this good rating in Figure 2.5:

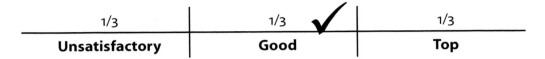

Figure 2.5

In this example, we used three critical few factors and gave them equal weight. In practice, you might have two, four or more. Do not use many. You want these to be the easy to remember for your employees. You might use different weights, as well, for example 50% for results, 25% for development and 25% for teamwork.

You will probably find yourself getting more specific too. For example, if all your results are customer service results, you will want to use the words "Customer Service" instead of the generic "results." If your teamwork is cross training and backing up others, then you may want to use those words. Do keep it simple and clear.

By the way, when you do get around to doing the ratings, stick to the way you told your employees you were going to do them. For example, rating someone a top performer who ignored teamwork and development, despite all your reminders, sends the message to others that teamwork and development don't matter. Face it. Your actions told them as much. When you communicate the "critical few" and their weightings, be confident that those few are what you really value and will live with.

In conclusion, it is important to communicate detailed work expectations and how they fit into the critical few factors. Also, communicate how much weight you'll give these factors if you must do an overall performance rating at appraisal time.

Review Questions

1. What is the first step in the day-to-day performance management strategy?

2. List at least three benefits for having "a meeting of the minds" about employee work expectations between an employee and the supervisor.

3. What are the benefits of having an employee thoroughly understand their job authority and responsibility?

4. Describe the purposes of having good performance standards. Give benefit examples.

5. Describe the value of communicating ranges of performance when discussing work expectations.

6. How might the activities of setting work expectations be different in "Team Environment" vs. in a "Command-control environment?"

Chapter Two Learning Activities

Setting Expectations Workshop Introduction

When we set expectations, we typically accomplish the following:

➤ *Clarify the overall purpose of a work team*
➤ *Clarify the division-of-work within the team*
➤ *Clarify each member's responsibilities and tasks*
➤ *Clarify objectives, standards, and decision-making authority*

I. Here are practice exercises for this workshop activity. First choose if you want to do these activities by creatively constructing a fictitious work group that you supervise or by completing them for an actual work group you supervise, or have supervised. For example, names might be department names, such as Patient Intake Department, Graphics Design Department, Accounts Payable Department, Help Desk, Product Engineering Team, Assembly, and so on. Write the group name next to your choice:

Fictitious work group name ＿＿＿＿＿＿＿＿＿＿＿＿＿, or

Actual work group name ＿＿＿＿＿＿＿＿＿＿＿＿.

II. Now answer #1 and #2 for your <u>work group or team</u>:

1. Describe your work team's primary objective in the fewest words possible.

2. Understand your work team's sub-tasks

Draw a pie chart with each pie slice representing a major result area or responsibility of your team or employee group.

III. Now that we've described the team, pick one job within the group or team and complete #'s 3 through 9.

3. Outline responsibilities and priorities for one employee job, give it a job title, and answer the questions that follow.

Job Title _____

3a. Select an employee job, and then draw a pie chart of that job. This time, try to use larger and smaller "pie pieces" to represent priorities.

3b.What is (are) the reason(s) for setting the priorities as you did?

3c. Would the person doing the job be able to state the same priorities as yours? Why, or why not?

3d. What will you do to get a "meeting of the minds" with the employee regarding priorities?

4. Outline objectives and standards

Clarity, measurability, and accountability are the tests of well-stated work objectives. The more clear, accountable, and measurable objectives are, the more motivational value they will have for employees.

Work objectives commonly are communicated via an "objective statement" or "key tasks statement." These statements will have the following elements:

- ➤ An action
- ➤ An expected result
- ➤ A time span or time frame
- ➤ A statement of people and other resources

Write an objective activity

Choose a high priority result or responsibility area from the pie chart. Write one objective for results expected for that segment of responsibility. In actual practice, there may be multiple objectives for each segment. Write your objective statement below.

5. Write out an example of a quantifiable or easy-to-measure standard.

6. Create an example of a hard-to-measure standard such as a result description or a general description.

7. Behavioral Descriptions Exercise

If you'll recall from the text, behavioral descriptions are concrete descriptions of desirable (or undesirable) behaviors such as initiative, being a team player, and so on. Try this brief exercise to learn how a supervisor might develop a set of descriptions or standards to judge a team member's performance. This may be done in a brainstorming group.

Activity: Recall a great team member and describe what behaviors—the things they said or did—gave you your high opinion. Write out specific behaviors that clarify each of the following general terms:

Cooperation –

Example: "On this team, we like to see cooperation. By cooperation I mean, if I see you offering to help others solve their problems or willingly giving help when asked, I'll think that is cooperation." (Offering help and giving help are observable behaviors.)

Initiative –

Team player –

Positive attitude –

8. The "Critical Few" Exercise

As a supervisor, keep the big picture in front of an employee in order to avoid misunderstandings when you get to the performance appraisal later on.

Describe or outline the "critical few" categories for a job, or responsibility, you have held. If you want, you may use *results, teamwork*, and *development* as your critical few categories. To clarify, give an example of specific work activities or responsibilities that might fall under each of the categories.

Optional Role Play

Pick a partner and work with them to role play communicating work expectations. Use the suggested steps given below and your ideas from numbers 1 through 8. One person should play the supervisor, the other plays the employee. Remember your purpose here is to practice the communication, not win an acting award. If you think you could do something better, try it again until you feel comfortable.

Switch roles and repeat until both understand the requirements of the job.

Here are suggested steps for conducting a meeting to communicate work expectations:

1. *Open the discussion*

2. *Define areas of responsibilities*

3. *Establish priorities*

4. *Clarify objectives and standards*

5. *Check for mutual understanding*

6. *Identify areas where training and coaching will be necessary. Agree to meet again to set goals and standards for the training needs.*

9. Relating objectives and standards

Now return to your objective statement(s), and outline standards that will help you and others know if performance is meeting or exceeding expectations. You may want to use the following format shown in Figure 2.7:

Objective	Standard	Review Mechanism	Authority
1.			
2.			
3.			

Figure 2.7

Topic Paper: Setting Work Expectations

Suggested Requirements

> Length: 2-4 pages double-spaced.
> Express main ideas with bullet points, numbered responses and simple, clear language. Show examples.
> Demonstrate understanding of the basic concepts of the chapter.
> Demonstrate imagination and creativity in setting expectations.
> Use this opportunity to apply performance management skills to a daily life situation.

Case of the Starter Castle

You own a home, actually a "starter castle," on a 20-acre lot in a very prestigious neighborhood. You live there with your spouse, children, and pets—two prize-winning, pet show dogs.

The estate consists of the main house, a four car garage, kennel, and small equipment shed for lawn mowers and garden equipment. Surrounding the house are large lawn and garden areas that must be maintained.

Your home's appearance is reputed to be the standard for the community. Because you are a licensed residential and landscape architect, this reputation is critical to your success. During the summer, you and your family will be leaving town on a two-month world tour, but the pet dogs will stay home.

You've hired Harry to "look after" the place and the dogs while you are away. He will have to shop at local stores and utilize the community's home services companies, vets, landscapers and so on. You will give him some level of authority to make decisions and spend money. You've provided him with a reasonable budget.

You must set clear work expectations for him, as you will be able to call in only once every 10 days. He is trustworthy and generally qualified for this work.

1. Write a paragraph further describing the specifics of the estate as you imagine it.

2. Describe Harry's overall job purpose or mission. (Remember that a mission statement should be very concise and help Harry understand his job from a "big picture" perspective. It provides a context for other goals and standards you might set for Harry.)

3. Imagine and list five key responsibilities for Harry's job. Rank the responsibilities as high, medium, or low priority.

4. Define decision-making authority levels for Harry in each or your areas of responsibility. (It is OK if a single authority description applies to more than one area.)

5. Choose one of Harry's responsibilities that is easy to measure, and write one properly-stated job objective.

6. Consider the job objective you just wrote and, with the concept of ranges of performance in mind, complete the following statement, "Performance is up to expectation when…"

7. Create a result description standard for any area of Harry's performance.

8. Create a general description standard for any area of Harry's performance.

9. Create *two* behavioral description standards for Harry's performance when he is working with others in the community.

10. Describe the "critical few" result areas you will use to measure Harry's overall performance for bonus pay when you return. What types of goals and standards might each cover?

Chapter Three

Understanding Two Important People Skills for Solving Performance Problems

Chapter Objectives

When you have finished the reading, you should be able to:

- ➤ State the difference between descriptive and evaluative feedback
- ➤ Construct descriptive feedback statements
- ➤ Offer constructive criticism
- ➤ Use both direct and non-direct probing styles
- ➤ Discover the behavioral effects of direct and non-direct probing techniques

Quick Review

Now that we know how to set performance expectations, and before we learn to analyze performance problems, let's learn the communication skills we'll need. Again, our three steps are:

- ➤ Set expectations
- ➤ Monitor and analyze performance
- ➤ Correct performance

Feedback and Probing: Two Important People Skills

To be effective when managing performance, supervisors must master two interpersonal skills: giving performance *feedback* and *probing*.

Giving feedback is an essential corrective technique. Not only is employee feedback a corrective technique by itself, but also we will use it later when we consider how to train, coach, counsel, and discipline.

Probing is useful to gain the information we need to solve problems, coach, and counsel. We'll explore it shortly.

Positive and Negative Feedback

Feedback can be positive—"good job"—or negative—"This needs to change." It is an important skill and critical for effective management. Good supervisors are reflexively proficient at giving feedback. Feedback is an ongoing two-way communication. It is more like a mirror that reflects a person's performance than it is a judgment. Feedback gives the employee information about their performance.

Supervisors rarely have difficulty giving positive feedback such as telling someone their work is exemplary. Positive feedback is identifying a situation or a behavior and reinforcing it through specific acknowledgment and approval. In other words, most people tend to repeat the things for which we receive positive feedback, praise, or recognition. Perhaps, the biggest difficulty for supervisors is remembering to give it.

Giving negative feedback about performance shortcomings or missed opportunities is more of a challenge. Negative feedback is identifying a situation or behavior requiring improvement. Here we address important aspects of giving negative, or as some call it, constructive feedback. What is the best way to give negative feedback? Let's look at two types.

The Two Types of Negative Feedback: Descriptive and Evaluative

While you may not know these two types of feedback by name, you've probably received both at some point, and, if you're like most people, you have a distinct preference.

Consider these two examples:

"Jim, you are at the center of all my problems as a supervisor. Why can't you just stay out of trouble? I mean, there were all those mistakes this week ... Then, well, I think I remember more from a couple of weeks ago. Why do you keep screwing up all the time?"

"Jim, I noticed that several production problems coming from your work station. The first was a part missing on Tuesday morning. The second was bad calibration on three units Wednesday afternoon; and the third was a series of cracked wiring brackets on Thursday. This caused four expensive reworks at the install sites."

Both of these are negative feedback, but which example do you think was descriptive and which was evaluative? In the first, the supervisor *evaluated* Jim's behavior (and not too fairly) and in the second, the supervisor simply and factually *described* Jim's performance results or behaviors. Thus, we call the second *descriptive feedback*.

As you may have guessed by now, supervisors do well to stick with descriptive feedback. This type of feedback is nothing more than describing to the employee the current level of performance as well as the effects. As mentioned before, the descriptive feedback technique is one that will show up in other corrective techniques as well, so master it.

You will notice from the example above that descriptive feedback is purely informational, and not emotional in nature. Research has shown that evaluative feedback causes a negative emotional response, or defensiveness, in the listener. (This started around the time that the supervisor in the first example said, "Jim, you are at the center of all my problems . . .")

This defensiveness blocks effective communication. How cooperative is Jim going to feel after being on the receiving end of such a tactless personal affront? Descriptive feedback tends to minimize defensive posturing and is a much better, more positive approach to beginning performance changes. When giving a typist descriptive feedback, the supervisor would say, "Mary, I noticed three typos in this memo," as opposed to, "Mary, you sure make a lot of careless mistakes." The "I message" is perceived as reporting information that focuses on the observed problem or behavior, while the "you message" is perceived as attacking, and focuses on the person, not the problem.

Again, look at the two examples about Jim. In the first example, the supervisor is being about as vague as it is possible to be. The supervisor and Jim could throw around heated generalities for half an hour just from that one comment and get nowhere. In the second example, the supervisor is very specific: a part missing on Tuesday morning, bad calibration on Wednesday, and so on. Jim will understand that these are factual statements and may even be able to recall specific events.

Timely feedback reinforces its importance. The sooner it's done the better it is. In the second example, you will notice that the feedback to Jim is timely, all centering on events occurring over the past week. In the first example, you get the sense that the only thing keeping the supervisor from dredging up every last thing he could on Jim was a memory that wasn't as good as it used to be. A statement such as, "Jim, three months ago you soldered a part in backwards," is not helpful from a control standpoint, nor is it timely enough to be useful.

Good feedback is brief and not lengthy. Consider this statement: "Amber, last month there were 11 things you did wrong. First, you made decaf coffee instead of regular for the morning meeting. Then you sent the Connelly invoice to the Smiths. Third, you forgot to put the Zelinsky file back in alphabetical order—I finally found it between Samson and Sandusky. Fourth . . ." I think you get the picture. Amber doesn't want to hear that and most of the incidents she won't be able to change now anyway. As a rule, people can't handle any more than two bits of negative feedback at one time.

Good feedback focuses on the effect *on the work and others* rather than the cause. Certainly, you want to avoid discussing your thoughts on the employee's character or personality. Evaluating the employee's life style, character, or personality is very personal and likely to cause defensiveness. Supervisors are concerned about performance behavior and not on changing a person's personality dynamics. It is best to leave that task to other professionals.

Communicating effects on the work and others has another big advantage. It clarifies your positive motives for the discussion. Everyone knows that the supervisor's job is to help get the work out. *Without your having to say as much, the effect statement tells the listener why you are having the conversation.* You are having the conversation simply because it affects the work, and part of any supervisor's job is to facilitate positive performance.

Take the case of tardy Joe: "Joe, I noticed that you were late three times so far this week: ten minutes on Monday, fifteen minutes on Tuesday, and over an hour this morning. To make up for it, Mary had to drop what she was doing and fill in. She now has to rush an important proposal estimate." Good supervisors focus on the effects of problems, and should seek causes, or ask "why" this is a problem, only if they suspect the problem is something that could be resolved with training.

Being late for work is hardly a training problem here, and that rushing proposal estimates can cause serious problems later on. The reason Joe is listening to this conversation is that it affects the work, not because the supervisor is being hard to please or some other capricious reason.

There are dramatic situations where immediate action is required. Even in the case of someone returning from lunch drunk, be descriptive. For example, "Larry, I smell alcohol on your breath. Safety policy requires me to arrange a taxi immediately to take you home." Common sense should tell us that this is not the best time to voice your opinion about Larry's drinking habits.

Descriptive vs. Evaluative Feedback Compared[iii]

Figure 3.1 compares descriptive and evaluative feedback and could make a good "reminder card" or summary of the key factors for good feedback.

Use Descriptive Feedback		Avoid Evaluative Feedback
Statements often begin with "I"	Vs.	Statements often begin with "You"
Perceived as reporting	Vs.	Perceived as attacking
Focuses on a problem or behavior	Vs.	Focuses on a person
Stresses the effect	Vs.	Stresses the cause
Specific	Vs.	General
Timely	Vs.	Untimely
Brief	Vs.	Lengthy

Figure 3.1

Two Common Mistakes

A common mistake when giving feedback is saying too much. Sometimes we feel compelled to expand simple feedback into a full-blown counseling or coaching discussion by asking questions. Resist urges to lecture and probe if you are giving a simple bit of feedback. You want the listener to process the information before you give them something else to think about.

For example, "John, I've noticed you drive the forklift too fast. This morning you almost hit Pat." This is a good place to pause, or stop, and let John think about it. Avoid skipping the "thinking time" and continuing with something like, "We cannot afford to have an accident. Please slow down and drive more carefully." Let's give John some credit. If he is at all reasonable, he knows he doesn't want to hurt someone else. He knows you can't afford accidents, and he knows that you want him to slow down. If he mentions he was violating the safety rules, all you have to do is agree with him that he is; and restate what they are.

Again, asking "Why?" is a mistake. Let's look at this example. "Jessie, I noticed that you were late returning from breaks the last two days. Why are you late getting back?" Asking the question, "Why?" invites excuses and defensiveness. It is likely Jessie will try to find some excuse, no matter how weak, to rationalize the lateness. Jessie is not likely to say a number of things that might be true, such as, "I'm late because I hate this job and I'm bored to death. That's why I stretch my breaks." Again, it is better to clarify the effects of the lateness on the work and on other employees. In other words if the performance issue would go away if the employee wanted it to, avoid asking why.

Of course, if you have to give the same employee the same message repeatedly, then you are moving into coaching, counseling or disciplinary discussions that we address later. You will use descriptive feedback as part of those messages, too. You will use your probes, suggestions, and advice there. Remember for now, we are addressing feedback as a communication technique, which is useful by itself as well.

Most Feedback Isn't Criticism

Thus far, we have been focusing on giving an employee negative feedback; an act some people would consider criticism. *It usually isn't.* Descriptive feedback is simply stating what you see going on and its effects. While this feedback is assertive, the intention is not to criticize, judge, or condemn.

Let's go to the dictionary to nail down what we mean by criticism. Criticism means *to find fault with openly*. A synonym for it is to *censure* which carries a strong suggestion of authority and of reprimanding. With these meanings floating around in the back of people's minds, it is easy to understand that receivers of criticism might take it personally and have strong emotional reactions to it. In addition, if you view all feedback as reprimanding or finding fault openly, you might be reluctant to give it.

This is a mistake. Be confident that timely descriptive feedback, properly given, is not the same as criticism. It is easy to see as well that evaluative feedback is more likely to be received as criticism. Let's compare two different wordings for the same performance message.

Good statement that describes:

> "I saw that on Tuesday, Wednesday and today your assignments were not completed on time. That delayed report delivery to the team and slowed production causing us to miss two important deadlines."

Poor statement that evaluates:

> "You have not been completing your work on time and you consistently whining about having too much to do. If you would just do the work and stop complaining about it all the time, you wouldn't have any late assignments, and I wouldn't have a production mess to clean up."

It is easy to see that the second evaluative statement is more likely to be received as criticism, with a large measure of emotion blended in with the words. As a supervisor, there may be times to criticize and reprimand. However, you will give descriptive feedback messages far more frequently; and they are emotion neutral.

Suggestions when Communicating Criticism

In those rare situations where you do intend to criticize, here is a suggestion that might help the discussion go more smoothly. Give the descriptive feedback information first, and then discuss your feelings about the situation, second. It is best to discuss your feelings and possible relationship effects separately from the task information. In other words, "Here is the information," and then, "Here is how I feel about it." Notice you are still speaking for yourself and not attacking them. To you, your feelings are facts.

Think through the following questions and suggestions before giving criticism. These should help you prepare. Over your career, they will become second nature for you.

1. Are they open to receive criticism right now? If not, schedule a better time.

2. Am I in the right frame of mind to give helpful criticism? If not, you may just vent your anger and make the situation worse.

3. Do we have enough time to discuss my concern? Do not bring it up if you don't have time to deal with an unexpected reaction.

4. Has the other person heard this criticism a number of times before? That brings the criticism into the possible realm of disciplinary action, and is more serious.

5. Have I criticized them before about this? Now this is more serious, since they apparently did not think change mattered.

6. Can they do anything about it? If you are about to criticize them for something they can't control, perhaps you should rethink what might be the real problem.

7. How might this criticism benefit them? Try to clarify how know-ing the effect of their behavior could help them.

8. Am I really trying to help the other person? Your positive mo-tives will be reflected in your tone of voice and nonverbal cues.

Also before criticizing others, you may want to ponder these quotations.

> *"Everything that irritates us about others can lead us to an understanding of ourselves."—Carl Gustav Jung*

> *"I've learned that people will forget what you said, people will forget what you did, but people will never forget how you made them feel."* — *Maya Angelou*

To review, most feedback a supervisor gives is not criticism. Effective nega-tive feedback is simply describing what you see going on and its effects. While descriptive feedback is assertive, the intention is not to criticize or evaluate.

By the way, if you think there are situations where descriptive feedback is too weak to be effective, you are right. *That doesn't mean, however, that the best next step is criticism.* Later, we will address counseling, discipline, and some other stronger measures.

Probing to Solve Problems

Probing can be a great way to get information from other people, a skill you will find crucial when supervising. There is power in information and, thus, people sometimes like to hold onto it or are afraid to reveal it. The techniques outlined in this chapter will enhance your ability to gather the necessary in-formation and discern whether what you thought you heard was, in fact, the message they meant to communicate.

Direct Questions

See if you can spot a pattern in the following three questions:

1. Do you have a driver's license?

2. Holly, can you drive a truck?

3. David, was the question I just asked you clear?

All three questions have a yes or a no answer. They are examples of the direct questioning technique—direct questions, direct responses. Direct questions are great tools for a supervisor: the questions are quick and usually yield a yes or no answer, they give the supervisor immediate feedback, and focus on a single issue.

Like any other form of communication, direct questioning has its limitations. Direct questions are best suited to situations when you must determine if you have been clearly understood and you need the immediate feedback of a yes or no answer. These questions are also useful in obtaining preliminary information that you can later verify by checking documents or with simple direct observation.

Direct questions are not suitable for assessing work attitudes or preferences. If you were to ask, "Do you like your job here? Yes or no," the employee working may rightly resent it. The question sounds as though you must either love the company or ship out.

They are also not appropriate for getting at facts or problems—in these applications, direct questions have all the warmth and tact of a military interrogation. Direct questions create defensiveness if we use them to question work performance or professional competency, and they are of no value at all in determining what went wrong after the fact. So what do we do then?

Non-Directive Communication Techniques

Obviously, as communicators we need facts to solve problems. We need facts to evaluate performance levels, consult, and stay generally informed. So how should we communicate with our employees in these situations? And how do we check what we've heard to be sure that it's what the employee meant to say?

In these and many more situations, we use what we call non-directive communication techniques. Here are some examples of non-directive techniques:

➤ Open-ended questions
➤ Laundry lists
➤ Supposing
➤ Echoing
➤ Reassuring

As we proceed through the non-directive techniques, remember that we can use them in endless situations and in endless combinations. If used properly, they'll yield abundant information, help us to test what we've heard, and ultimately make our jobs easier as supervisors.

Open-Ended Questions

1. "How do you feel about what happened?"

2. "What kind of job would you like?"

3. "Why do you think we're having this problem?"

4. "Which two employees do you think would be best suited for this assignment?"

Go back and look again at the words that begin open-ended questions: how, what, why, which. Notice that, in the first example, the questioner is asking for information—to answer the question, the receiver must respond with something more than a yes or no.

In the second example, the questioner is asking for choices or preferences by inquiring what kind of job the receiver would like. When the receiver has answered, the questioner can follow up with more pointed questions, such as, "Why would you like that particular job?"

How would a direct question have been less effective in that situation? Suppose the questioner had asked "Would you like a job here?" or "Would you like to be in administrative work?" Can you see how the answers to those direct questions would yield much less information?

Recall the third example, which posed the question, "Why do you think we're having this problem?" Notice how the question is formulated to ask for opinions, judgments, and facts. The question shows respect and a sense of value for the receiver and is a much better question than "Did you cause this problem," or "Who caused this problem?"

The fourth example asks, "Which two employees would be best suited for this assignment?" Starting a question with "which," is another way of asking for the receiver's judgment. Consider the alternative, "Is Fred a better worker than John?" That question has trouble written all over it.

From the examples you can see that open-ended questions help maintain a neutral, non-emotional climate where communication can occur without fear or inhibition. By using open-ended questions, the questioner avoids "telegraphing" a preferred response—the questioner will have the opportunity to hear the recipient's actual thoughts on the matter.

How, what, why, which—this is how we ask open-ended questions.

Laundry Lists

Laundry lists are just what the name implies—the questioner strings out a series of choices or possibilities, much like laundry hanging on a line, and asks the receiver to respond.

Following are three examples:

1. "There are three shifts we have: 8:00-4:00, 4:00-12:00, and 12:00-8:00. Which is best for your schedule?"

2. "What do you see as your main problem: turnover, absenteeism, or inconsistent work?"

3. "Would you prefer to work on your own, be part of a group, or have more contact with the public?"

Laundry lists force the receiver to choose by stating a preference among alternatives. They are valuable in helping others see beyond a single issue, problem, or choice. By posing questions in this way, we afford ourselves the opportunity to hear the pros and cons of a particular choice. Laundry list questions allow the questioner to evaluate the reasoning behind the receiver's selection. As with open-ended questions, laundry lists can provide us with a good deal of information.

Supposing

Supposing is useful in at least two common supervisory situations. First, it gives the questioner and receiver a chance to change roles, offering the receiver the opportunity to step aside and think from a different point of view. This will often give the receiver valuable perspective on a situation. Here are some examples:

1. "If you were me, Sam, how would you handle this situation?"

2. "Suppose you could be Eileen for moment; how would you feel right now?"

3. "Suppose we had a reduction in staff; how would we get the work done?"

4. "If we could do it over again, how would we do it?"

Notice that all four examples start with two words: "if" and "suppose." Starting the question with "if" or "suppose" makes the question a hypothetical one and opens up an interesting thought exercise for the receiver that will often be quite illuminating. By asking the receiver to step into someone else's shoes, ("If you were me, Sam" and "Suppose you could be Eileen for a moment") the questioner asks the receiver to consider the feelings or predicament of another person. This may lead the receiver to feel more empathy for a co-worker or consider what he or she might do to help alleviate the problem.

Second, it is also useful to explore thinking about solution alternatives. For example, "If we were to expand the sales territory, what effect might we see on revenue and travel expense?"

Echoing

Can you recall a time when you've spoken in a cave or a tunnel and heard your voice come cascading back to you? The words were yours, but they sounded funny, and may have caused you to think twice about what you said. The echoed words shifted the communication dynamic as you changed from the speaker to the listener and began to evaluate the statement you heard.

Our fourth non-direct communication technique, echoing, works on the same principle. Consider this example between a distraught employee and her supervisor.

> Employee: "I'm *so* fed up with this job. I think I'm going to quit."
> Supervisor: "You think you're going to *quit*?"
> Employee: "Oh, I don't know—the situation has me very upset. I guess I shouldn't quit over it, I just don't know what to do."

This employee doesn't really want to quit her job. Mostly, she just wants to vent her frustrations, be heard, and try to find solutions to the problem. By echoing her statement, the employee's supervisor is helping her understand her feelings about a problem.

When the employee hears her own statement coming back to her, her less emotional side returns and she can begin to regain some objectivity on the issue.

By echoing, the supervisor is letting the employee know that he or she is actively listening, has received the message, and understands its importance.

Here is another use of the echoing technique:

Employee: "I don't have anything else to say. This whole problem is Caroline's fault."

Supervisor: "The *whole* problem is Caroline's fault?"

Employee: "Well I don't know if the whole problem is, but certainly some of it."

The supervisor is echoing to test the accuracy of the information: is it really, all Caroline's fault? By doing this, the supervisor is asking the employee to verify the information by sending it back again.

If you're stumped and looking for a way to echo, try starting with, "In other words, what you mean is . . ." or "If I understand you correctly, what you said was . . ."

Bottom line: echoing is an excellent way for the questioner to test the accuracy of what was said, and what they think they heard.

Reassurance

Employee: "I guess I said everything I should. I don't think there's anything more to say.

Supervisor: "Well, I understand how you feel. We've been talking now for quite a while, but if there's anything else bothering you, I'd like to hear that too. Why don't we talk a little more?"

Unlike the first four non-direct techniques, reassurance is not designed to gain new information only. Its primary usefulness is in keeping a difficult dialogue moving forward for insight and detail. Many times—particularly during performance reviews or performance counseling sessions—employees will hesitate and have a fear of saying too much or, perhaps, the wrong thing.

Here's another example of how reassurance can help an employee continue his or her communication with you:

Employee: "I'm so angry you can't know how I feel."

Supervisor: "I have feelings too. I can understand that."

Employee: "You wouldn't understand it . . . I wouldn't expect you to . . . You couldn't understand how I feel."

Supervisor: "Actually, Joe, I've felt like that myself many times."

So what does reassurance have in common with open-ended questions, laundry lists, supposing, and echoing? All are forms of active listening. All assure the sender that we are both listening and empathizing with the feelings behind the messages. All say to the sender, "Go ahead and talk. You can tell me. I will listen and understand." More importantly, all the techniques communicate that "I care, both about your message, and about your feelings."

Who do you talk to when you have a problem? Who do you think will listen and, hopefully, understand? Odds are good that you will seek out someone who will reassure you and help you feel that things will be OK. Reassurance is one of the subtlest and most important communication techniques, one that the effective communicator will use again and again. So, remember to use these words:

- ➤ OK
- ➤ All right
- ➤ I see
- ➤ Tell me more

By doing so, you send a signal that the sender has nothing to fear and that it is safe to continue.

In summary, these are the five major non-directive communications techniques:

1. Open-ended questions: questions that begin with how, what, why, which

2. Laundry lists: questions which present choices, options, or alternatives

3. Supposing: questions which allow the other person to step aside, change roles, to explore someone else's attitudes or point of view

4. Echoing: sending back the message to test whether what you heard is what the sender really meant

5. Reassurance: comforting words that express concern for the sender, the message, and the feelings behind the message

Review Questions

1. What are the likely negative effects when a supervisor uses evaluative feedback instead of descriptive feedback?

2. Describe how descriptive feedback is different from criticism.

3. Identify situations where direct probes can be effective.

4. Identify situations where it is best to use non-directive probing techniques.

Chapter Three Learning Activities

1. Descriptive Feedback Exercises

Create a properly worded descriptive feedback statement for each of the following situations. Use language that is specific, brief, and clear. Be sure to include an "effect statement."

    a)   An employee is not completing assignments on time and constantly complains that they have too much to do.

    b)   An employee is a real "lead foot" on the forklift, and now has had a near miss.

    c)   An employee has been continuously late returning from their breaks.

    d)   An employee is failing to meet output expectations on a regular basis.

    e)   You observed an employee arguing with a customer.

    f)   Write out a descriptive feedback statement for a life situation where you have avoided giving someone feedback.

    Descriptive Feedback Role Play (Optional)

    Meet with another person and each take a turn at role-playing a descriptive statement, from one of the above. Discuss results and difficulties.

2. Probing Techniques Exercise One

Following is a list of single-choice questions. Read the question and choose the correct questioning technique out of the options listed below each question. Indicate the correct answer by circling, highlighting, or putting an "x."

    1.   Are you able to work nights?
        a.   open-ended question
        b.   direct question

    c. laundry list

    d. supposing

2. Which of your employees could fill in?

    a. laundry list

    b. open-ended question

    c. supposing

    d. echoing

3. If you were John, what would you do now?

    a. laundry list

    b. supposing

    c. open-ended question

    d. echoing

4. Would you prefer typing, filing, or public contact?

    a. laundry list

    b. direct question

    c. open-ended question

    d. supposing

5. OK, good. Tell me more about that.

    a. echoing

    b. open-ended question

    c. reassurance

    d. supposing

6. In other words, Sam refused your instruction?

    a. echoing

    b. supposing

    c. laundry list

    d. open-ended question

7. Why do you think you'd like this job?

    a. echoing

    b. open-ended question

    c. laundry list

    d. supposing

8. If you were Bill, how would you feel now?
   a. supposing
   b. reassurance
   c. open-ended question
   d. laundry list

9. Is lack of staff, poor morale, or absenteeism the major problem here?
   a. open-ended question
   b. supposing
   c. laundry list
   d. direct question

10. Don't stop talking, I want to hear more.
    a. echoing
    b. reassurance
    c. supposing
    d. open-ended question

11. Do you like to work weekends?
    a. open-ended question
    b. supposing
    c. direct question
    d. laundry list

12. In other words, you want to quit?
    a. supposing
    b. echoing
    c. direct question
    d. reassurance

13. What would you recommend we do?
    a. direct question
    b. open-ended question
    c. reassurance
    d. laundry list

14. Which of your neighbors do you like?
    a. direct question
    b. laundry list

   c.   open-ended question
   d.   supposing

15. What do you see as the reasons Fred quit?
   a.   direct question
   b.   open-ended question
   c.   supposing
   d.   reassurance

3. Probing Techniques Exercise Two

Read and compare the following two discussions, Allan and Joe, Turnover – Discussion One and Discussion Two, and answer the following two questions:

1.   Which discussion is more effective?
2.   What caused the difference?

Participants:
       Supervisor: Allan
       Assistant: Joe

Allan and Joe, Turnover - Discussion One

Allan: Joe, I've noticed that we've got a lot of people quitting on the shift that you work.

Joe: Oh?

Allan: Yes, are you doing anything to make people want to leave?

Joe: No. What makes you think I do?

Allan: I don't know, I was just wondering. Do you know why everybody's quitting?

Joe: No.

Allan: Do you yell at them or do anything like that?

Joe: No.

Allan: You're not too rough on the younger ones or anything, are you?

Joe: No.

Allan: Well, it beats me. I can't figure out why they're quitting, and you don't seem to know. Maybe it's just a coincidence?

Joe: That's probably it.

Allan and Joe, Turnover - Discussion Two

Allan: Hi, Joe. How's it going?

Joe: Not bad.

Allan: Boy, that's bravery.

Joe: What do you mean?

Allan: You must be up to your eyeballs with all the turnover you've had lately.

Joe: Yeah, that's true.

Allan: Where's everybody going? Migrating south for the winter?

Joe: Oh, it's just kids these days. You know how they are.

Allan: What do you mean?

Joe: Can't depend on them—they want to get paid for doing nothing.

Allan: Well, I can sympathize with you. I know you wouldn't tolerate that.

Joe: You bet I don't. One time late and I warn them. Twice and they're out.

Allan: You've had to fire that many?

Joe: No. Usually they quit before I get the chance.

Allan: In other words, they're all quitting on you?

Joe: That's right. Can you believe that? They say they don't like the way I talk to them! What nerve, those good for nothings!

Allan: Hey, wait. Good for nothings? You really think so?

Joe: Well, I didn't mean that.

Allan: Maybe you didn't mean it, but that's what you said. You were coming on pretty strong, Joe. Maybe you're coming on too strong with them. I mean, maybe stronger than you think.

Joe: You might have a point there.

Allan: Look, Joe—it's a lot of pressure, workin' this place. I guess a guy can start overreacting to things and he might not even know it. I mean, I'm not you, but do you think that could be happening to you?

Joe: That could be. I guess I've been under a lot of stress lately.

Allan: Joe, you're a good man, I'm sure you can handle it. But if you can't, you let me know, OK? Maybe I can help. We could get Jerome to watch your shift for a couple of days; maybe you could go fishing for a bit, get some time away.

Joe: Thanks, I appreciate that. You're a real stand-up guy, Allan.

Again, the two questions to be answered are

1. Which discussion is more effective?
2. What caused the difference?

Chapter Four,

Deciding How to Handle Performance Problems

Chapter Objectives

When you have finished the reading, you will be able to:

- ➤ Apply stating performance problems properly
- ➤ Apply a performance problem analysis technique
- ➤ Differentiate between training and motivation problems

Handling Performance Problems

In Chapter Two, we learned how to set performance expectations. In this chapter and the next, we introduce what to do if an employee's performance does not measure up to expectation. In other words, how will we handle performance problems and issues? Before looking at training techniques, motivation problems, and employee development in general, we will look at a performance analysis model.

Problem Statements Do Not Include Causes or Solutions

A performance problem is the difference, or gap, between current performance and expected performance. Let's look at a couple of examples that we will reexamine in more detail later.

> *Problem statement: The employee makes personal phone calls during work time when the expectation is to make personal calls during break time. Work is not done because of the personal phone calls during work.*

> *Problem statement: The employee uses more beads per gallon of paint than is recommended. We normally go through about 700-800 pounds per day. Currently, we are using about 1200-1400 pounds a day, which is nearly double the material.*

Each example describes a desired or expected situation and the current situation. A problem is simply the difference or gap. No*tice, we did not attempt to state possible causes or solutions in the problem statement.*

When stating a problem, it is best to use a situation description, as shown above, and avoid describing the problem in the wording of a solution. For example, *"The employee needs to handle personal problems before coming to work instead of making personal phone calls at work." While this may be true, stating it this way closes down thinking and opens the matter to defensiveness and argument.*

Perhaps a variation on second problem statement will make this point more clearly. Instead of the situation statement above, suppose the supervisor defines it as follows: *"The employee is being careless and wasting beads."* Here the supervisor blames the situation on the employee and closes down thinking about other causes. There could be many causes for the problem such as equipment problems, improper training, faulty beads, and so on.

Sticking to the current situation—expected situation model saves a lot of misunderstanding and opens thinking. For now, we will just assume that a performance problem exists, and we want to decide upon a strategy to eliminate it.

Analyzing Performance Problems: Can't Do/Won't Do Analysis[iv]

As supervisors, we have a number of performance-correcting techniques in our toolkit: motivating, coaching, counseling, job rotation or discipline, to name a few. With so many possibilities, how are we to know which is the right tool for the job? Fortunately, we can decide the best tools by using a simple, three-step process, shown in the following paragraphs and the accompanying chart.

Three-Step Performance Diagnostic Process

When faced with handling a performance problem, analyze the problem to help you decide on the best correcting strategy. *At this point, you only want to decide if the problem is important enough to do something about; and whether it is a skill or a motivation problem.* Later you will choose the specific correcting technique. Do the analysis by following these, three steps. Think through these steps in the order shown.

1. First, define the "problem statement." Describe the employee's current performance and the ways in which it does not meet expectations. Later, we will address the nature of performance problems in much more detail.

2. Second, decide if the problem is of urgent importance: if not, ignore, for now, and monitor the situation. Delay action to see if the problem recurs, gets more serious, or otherwise becomes important.

   The answer to this question can change as the situation changes. For example, if Pat is late for work once per year, the supervisor is not likely to think it is an important problem. If Pat begins arriving late for work every other day, the supervisor might conclude that the situation has changed, and has become an important problem.

3. Third, decide if the cause of the performance problem is a deficiency of skill or knowledge. Ask the following questions: Could the employee perform the task properly if it were the most important thing in their life? Could they perform as expected if motivation were perfect? If they could perform as expected, then they *know how* to do it.

For the most part, training will not solve motivation problems, and motivating will not solve training problems. One will encounter exceptions, but think carefully before deciding a situation to be an exception.

See Figure 4.1ᵛ for an illustration of the diagnostic process.

```
                    ┌─────────────────────┐
                    │      Step 1         │
                    │  Problem Statement  │
                    └─────────────────────┘
                              │
                              ▼
                                        No
                    ◇ Step 2  ◇ ──────────►   Ignore or
                      Important?                monitor
                              │
                             Yes
                              │
                              ▼
    Yes                                   No       Make
 Train/  ◄──────  ◇  Step 3  ◇  ──────────►    Performance
 Coach              Caused by a                   Matter
                      skill
 "Can't do"         deficiency?              "Won't do"
 problems                                     problems
```

We use training and development strategies to solve problems on this side. We call them "Can't do" or skill problems.

We use motivating strategies to solve problems on this side. We call them "Won't do" or willingness problems.

Figure 4.1

Methods for Handling *Can't Do* Problems

By looking at the bottom left of Figure 4.1, we see that the obvious strategy for skills or knowledge deficiency problems is to coach or to arrange training. In other words, if we answer, "yes" to the question, "Is the problem caused by a skill and knowledge deficiency?" then we would choose training or coaching techniques to eliminate the problem. We call them "Can't do" or skill problems.

The following is a list of methods for handling "can't do" problems. These are so important; we devote an entire chapter to them later.

Address "can't do" problems with

- Descriptive feedback
- Formal training
- Formal coaching
- On-the-job training (OJT)
- Coaching
- Substitute role
- Developmental job assignments
- Job rotation
- New hire orientation
- Job instruction training
- Reading programs

Methods for Handling Won't Do Problems[vi]

By looking at the bottom right of Figure 4.1, we see that the obvious strategy for problems *not* caused by a skill and knowledge deficiency is to make proper performance matter. In other words, if we were to answer "no" to the question, "Is the problem caused by a skill or knowledge deficiency?" then we would choose strategies aimed at making proper performance matter to the employee. This would be a motivation strategy. We call them "Won't do" or willingness problems. The following is a list of methods for handling "won't do" problems. These are so important; we devote an entire chapter to them later.

Address "won't do" problems with

- Descriptive feedback
- Motivating and ABC analysis
- Counseling
- Discipline
- Performance improvement plans

Usually, techniques used by the supervisor to solve "Won't Do" problems are done in a specific order, which may be determined by company policy. They are usually applied in the order shown above starting with feedback and proceeding to discipline or improvement plans.

Analysis Examples

Let's look at some examples from actual situations as described by their supervisors. To keep it simple for now, we will focus on just how to use the analysis model, and avoid getting into the specific actions to remedy these situations.

Situation 1:

> *As a Supervisor, I have a staff member who likes her email and phone a little too much. Every day when I come back from lunch I hear her quickly get off the phone with an "Oh, I better get back to work." When I approach her with this issue, she makes it a point to let me know she just got on the phone, and all her work for the day is caught up. She is my backup and there is always more work to do. When I talk to her about this it will improve for about a week, and then she goes back to her old habits.*

Analysis:

Problem statement: The employee makes personal phone calls during work time when the expectation is to make personal calls during break time. Work is not done because of the personal phone calls.

Is this problem important? Yes. Perhaps this would not be important if it happened rarely, but here is a chronic pattern of ignoring clear work expectations.

Is the cause of the problem a skill or knowledge deficiency? No. The employee could perform as expected if motivation were perfect. In other words, they could do it if they wanted to. After all, they get better for a week or so. There is no training problem here.

Conclusion: This is a "Won't Do" problem and the Supervisor has to take steps to make proper performance matter.

Situation 2:

An employee in their first year on the job is assigned to paint stripes on area roadways. The employee is motivated, and has had a great record in the past with different equipment.

When painting he uses almost 50% more reflective glass beads as a different employee did last time the roads were striped.

Analysis:

Problem statement: The employee uses more beads per gallon of paint than is recommended. We normally go through about 700-800 pounds per day. Currently, we are using about 1200-1400 pounds a day, at a cost of $ .34 per pound.

Is this problem important? Yes. Money is wasted and too many beads can cause dangerous road surfaces.

Is the cause of the problem a skill or knowledge deficiency? Yes. The Supervisor determined this is a "can't do" problem. He determined that the employee is trying his best, but he is not able to operate the equipment at the same speed the last employee operated it. He knows what button to push, or what knob to turn to make the equipment run, but he lacks enough experience to operate the machine at the most efficient speed.

Conclusion: This is a "can't do" problem and the supervisor will take steps to train or coach the employee.

Situation 3:

The employee that is reluctant to learn and perform new types of x-ray studies. This employee is an experienced technologist, probably 5 years from retirement. She completed the written portion of the training in a new procedure." Now it is time to complete the required on-the-job training portion of the training. She repeatedly comes up with excuses to not complete the on-the-job part. She says, "Today is not a good day, or I can't handle it today," and so on. The Supervisor hasn't pushed the issue in the past, but now needs all staff trained for better coverage.

Analysis:

> Problem statement: The employee is stalling completion of important training to perform the job duties. The Supervisor expects the employee to complete on-the-job training, and they have not done so.

> Is this problem important? Yes, the importance of this problem has increased. Fully trained staff members are now required for the workload.

> Is the cause of the problem a skill or knowledge deficiency? No.

> Conclusion: This is a "won't do" problem. The employee could schedule time to start the training if she wanted to. The Supervisor will take steps to make proper performance matter.

What Makes a Bad Employee?

Employee performance problems are to be expected and handled. When they think about it, few supervisors believe that employees come to work predisposed to be a bad employee. Most employees are fair, stable people who would like to do good work.

The purpose of the analysis model is not to label employees as good or bad. It is a way to decide the best approach to help the employee succeed and take pride in their work. Even good employees can have "can't do" or "won't do" problems at times. Good employees properly approached will cooperate to become better.

Here is a final word about "won't do" problems. Supervisors might prefer to handle training problems instead of motivation problems. They mistakenly think all "won't do" problems are nasty conflict situations involving disciplinary action or firing. While it is likely that ignoring problems can cause them to escalate to that level, they need not.

Many "won't do" problems are minor and easily corrected with information or feedback. Self-aware employees change their performance all the time without being told. In other words, they have the skills already, and adapt their performance to new information. For example, a supervisor gives an employee descriptive feedback about being on time for meetings. A reasonable employee starts to be on time. It was a "won't-do" problem easily remedied by feedback information. The problem is solved and soon forgotten.

Of course, there is a possibility of a truly bad employee who requires disciplinary action or termination. Perhaps "won't do" problems get a bad connotation because we tend to remember a conflict ridden discipline session and forget numerous problems briefly handled with a bit of feedback.

What's Next?

Now that we understand how to differentiate training and motivation problems, we look at how to eliminate or minimize their effect in following chapters.

Review Questions

1. What role do performance expectations have in specifying performance problems? In your response, include the general definition of a performance problem.

2. What are some questions to consider when deciding if a performance problem has a training cause or a motivation cause?

3. Identify at least four strategies for handling "can't do" problems.

4. Identify at least four strategies for handling "won't do" problems.

Chapter Four Learning Activities

1. For each of the following situations, label whether you think the situation likely represents a "can't do" or a "won't do" problem situation by writing either "can't do" or won't do" in the space.

_____1a. Hector is often late for a regularly scheduled meeting.

_____1b. Mary used to do an error-free job on the accounting report. Since changing to the new software, there are errors in her report.

_____1c. George was just assigned to the new test equipment and he is taking much longer to do the tests than his predecessor.

_____1d. The customer lines at her service counter have been much longer than acceptable after Joyce was "passed over" for promotion last week.

2. Write an example of a performance problem analysis using the Can't do—Won't do model in Figure 4.1. This could be at work, or outside of work. Please include the following:

2a. A properly stated description of the performance problem including a description of the current and expected levels of work performance.

2b. Discuss the importance question.

2c. Describe why you think it is either a "can't do" or a "won't do" problem?

2d. Comment on training or motivating strategies that might work.

3. Discuss how the importance of a problem can increase over time or as situations change.

Chapter Five
The Supervisor as a Trainer

Handling Can't Do Performance Problems through Employee Development

Chapter Objectives

When you have finished the reading, you will be able to:

> ➤ Consider a developmental perspective of supervising others
> ➤ Understand the four stages of job performance growth
> ➤ Understand the supervisor's role in employee development
> ➤ Differentiate between strategic and job-level training needs
> ➤ Choose training strategies that fit the employee's stage of job performance growth and development
> ➤ Determine development responsibilities
> ➤ Conduct a training needs analysis
> ➤ Identify formal and on-the-job training techniques
> ➤ Plan to apply basic training techniques such as an orientation plan and job instruction training plan

Do You Have a Developmental Perspective?

How do you view your role as a supervisor? Are you a coach or a cop? The average supervisor is better served by viewing themselves as a coach. This is not to say that you never have to "kick someone off the team," but much of what you do is training and informing.

Before getting into employee training and development in detail, let's look at a helpful viewpoint or perspective. This supervisory attitude is worth pausing to understand as it can be as important as training techniques themselves.

A *developmental perspective* is a philosophy of supervising others where the supervisors see the performance management part of their job as an opportunity to train, coach, develop, and guide employees. When interacting with employees, they look for opportunities to facilitate performance improvement.

In recent decades, there have been big changes in companies and other organizations. Management builds productivity through MIS[7]-based control systems, downsizing, moving toward high-participation work teams, implementing total-quality management, total-service management, and other approaches. New equipment and technologies force employee learning whether you are a huge corporation reengineering an entire production facility or a small business buying a new piece of equipment. These changes are necessary to compete and survive; and they require employees to learn. They drive supervisors see their jobs differently, too.

The right managerial outlook reduces conflict and sets the climate for co-operative performance management. Successful supervisors today adopt a *developmental perspective* or philosophy that differs from much of past thinking about how to manage. How might it differ? Let's review a little history so you can see if you are on the right track.

Older Perspectives by Comparison

In the mid to late 20th Century, only a few forward-looking organizations gave employee training and development the emphasis it needed. The majority of North American managers practiced command-control management where the manager did most of the thinking and issued the orders, tightly controlled and monitored progress, and periodically evaluated performance of their "subordinates." Even the classifying of employees as "subordinates" under-scored a "one-up, one-down" relationship. When the "subordinate" messed up, the supervisor put on the cop hat. A developmental perspective was not a common view of how one supervised others.

Were employees ever consulted? Sure, but the consultation was usually constrained, and a few cynics might say it was a manipulative "motivational trick." While these activities are not intrinsically unproductive, the dominant management culture, or perspective was still "command-control" and not developmental.

On the surface, the command-control perspective of management seemed to work well, which may have perpetuated the "cop" style. Matters did improve later on as the supervisor evolved to more of a "friendly, neighborhood cop," but a cop all the same. Capital, technological, and world market factors may have hidden any shortcomings of such management practices. Most companies overlooked the work of Mary Parker Follett (1868–1933) whose ideas introduced human psychology and human relations into industrial management. Instead, manufacturing settings were more influenced by the Scientific Management, the Process School of Management, and military command ideas. (Even these ideas were sometimes misapplied, but that is another story.)

How did managers and supervisors view employees? Was their managerial perspective a developmental one? There may be a contradiction between how past managers would verbally answer this question and how they would act day-to-day. If you were the proverbial mouse in the corner, you'd hear supervisors quite honestly say positive things about their employees and that employee development was important. However, if one watched their *behavior*, there was a contradiction. There was an invisible barrier between the "thinkers"—management—and the "doers"—employees. This was especially true during stressful business times.

Training and developing employees was peripheral to the main responsibilities of the supervisor. It was an activity, an event, an overhead cost item, a "flavor of the month" management fad, but not a pervasive way to supervise.

If this was a common worldview, then it must have had benefits. What were they? One benefit is tighter financial and production controls made possible by more centralized decision-making. Supervisors felt in control. (Whether or not they really were is another story, too.) Things could be more standardized, neater and cleaner. You might view workers as extensions of their production machines. Many jobs were kept routine and repetitive with limited job scope and depth.

Likely a company did well with this philosophy if it manufactured standard products to match standard customer requirements. Employees worked under a standard labor contract. Jobs were simple. The training and learning curve for an employee was short and steep. Employee training was not a large time or cost concern for supervisors. Unfortunately, for workers, robotics and cheap labor elsewhere have dissolved many of these jobs.

As the world and the work changed, this way of supervising began to falter. Supervisors ran into costly problems when they tried to apply older management practices to dynamic production systems requiring teamwork or to "knowledge workers."

Some costs are subjective and hard to quantify, but let's think about answers to some general questions:

➤ What are the costs of a great plan that the work team can't implement?
➤ What are the costs of employee suggestions never made?
➤ What are the costs of a lost customer because an employee mishandled a situation?
➤ What are the costs of using obsolete technologies because the work team doesn't know anything better?
➤ What are the costs of a good employee who leaves because they fear they are getting technically stale?
➤ How much does a bored, alienated, or resentful employee cost?

We could go on with other questions, but there is at least one other that we might consider: *How fair is it to me and my family that I have to work long hours and weekends because I'm doing work that employees on my team should do?* A supervisor can't delegate and empower if the employees aren't trained. If they can't delegate and empower, they can't manage their time effectively. In other words, if you want to manage your time, delegate. If you delegate, you must train and develop employees to handle things well.

It is fair to say that today's supervisor should be the coach and manage with a developmental perspective. The following list summarizes a few reasons why a developmental view of supervision is compelling:

> ➤ Rapid responses to production and customer demands require employees to make decisions as dictated by, and close to, the situation.
> ➤ More employees today are knowledge workers who know the technical aspects of their jobs better than their supervisors or managers.
> ➤ Continuing domestic and global competition requires continuous service, quality and productivity improvement.
> ➤ Today's employees need to adapt, cope, know, and use new systems and technologies.

A big part of the developmental perspective is the supervisor's belief that few employees get out of bed each day saying, "I hope I do a bad job at work today." Employees are concerned about getting proper orientation and job skills training. Most employees want to improve themselves in order to advance in their jobs, or enhance their careers, or simply have a more pleasant day free of stress or anxiety.

Are You the Coach?

Training and employee development is an important role for supervisors. Just like the sports coach, we have to get our team ready for the game. We want our team to get better each day. We might have to get new team members up to speed fast to replace or backup more experienced players. Whether or not the specific words are in the job description, supervisors are responsible for performance improvement, especially if the competing team is getting better or the plays more complex. Remember too, the team has to be ready for the challenges of "next year's season."

Employers are either moving forward or falling behind. They are never standing still. Training, education, and development, from an organizational viewpoint, are all concerned with growth or change. Here are two important definitions:

➤ Training is coaching a person to a proficient level of performance, usually with specialized instruction and practice.

➤ Education is a process of imparting general knowledge or skill systematically.

Both training and education involve learning. Development is the process of helping individuals to realize or expand their potentials, so that they use their abilities fully to satisfy themselves and the employer. A supervisor's commitment to training, education, and development reflects a developmental perspective.

Use a Problem-solving Style

Development-oriented supervisors adopt a problem-solving style. They see most performance problems as an opportunity to train, coach, develop, and guide. Employees respond by methodically improving.

Supervisors see performance problems as opportunities to demonstrate positive intentions and to help employees achieve their best possible performance level. The problem-solving approach creates a motivational effect that enhances employees' self-esteem and self-worth, as opposed to making people feel inadequate and fearful. After all, we all can improve. The compensation plan and the performance appraisal support by making performance improvement matter.

That's enough philosophy and coach vs. cop talk for now. Let's look at technique.

Handling "Can't Do" Performance Problems

For the remainder of this chapter, we will focus on "can't do" performance problems (and what supervisors and organizations can do about them). The methods for handling "won't do problems will be the focus of the next chapter. That topic will give us a chance to dust off the cop hat for a while, but for now, it is 100% coach hat.

"Can't do" performance problems limit performance of the entire organization. Let's examine that relationship to understand how it affects the supervisor.

Employee Development and Organizational Health

Organizations, like individuals, can exhibit various states of health. Some organizations are healthy, alive, and vibrant—they are exciting places to work. On the other hand, there are organizations that spend too much time on the couch eating potato chips—weak, tired, and struggling for survival.

Organizations are human inventions and, thus, people create states of organizational wellness and illness. Organizations, like people, can damage their health through lifestyle choices.

Let's say that Norm, 67, just had his first grandchild. He's a pack-a-day smoker, has a beer belly, and hasn't exercised regularly since the Carter administration. Norm decides he has to change his ways if he is going to see his granddaughter graduate from high school. Therefore, he kicks the cigarettes, cuts down to five beers a week, and takes up yoga. After a couple of months, he feels like a million bucks!

In the same way, organizations facing extinction can change their habits and practices to become more viable in the long term. One great way to do that is to grow through training and development.

Your Mission is to Improve Work Group Performance

As said before, training and development aims to improve employee performance. Supervisors at all levels of organizations monitor the performance and productivity of their work teams on a daily basis. Work group performance is the main mission.

First is a brief word of context. Training and development is the focus of this chapter, but is only part of the mix for solving performance problems. For example, training may help solve productivity improvement problems or adding additional technical capability to an organization. However, to solve these completely, other actions may be required. Examples include introducing new capital equipment, establishing a fitting organizational goal structure and management control system, setting up an effective workflow process, fitting job design, or hiring employees with capabilities to fit the task.

Any single factor, taken in isolation, will not give the supervisor enough information to ascertain the current level of performance and the team's potential. For example, even well trained employees cannot perform well in poorly designed jobs, or if their performance expectations are either too low or improperly communicated. They will not perform well if they lack the basic skills, experience, or training that their job requires. In addition, no one will work up to their potential if they are not motivated or have outdated tools.

Here we are addressing "can't do" performance problems. These performance problems have a training and development solution. Supervisors invest much time in training activities. To get results, someone needs to assume responsibility for growth and development.

Who Is Responsible?

Many people assume that the Training or Human Resources (HR or Personnel) Departments are responsible for training and development. This would be a misconception. While these departments provide valuable services, they rarely are the primary parties responsible for development in a supervisor's work group.

So who is responsible? Although this question may seem basic, many organizations are unclear about it. Is the supervisor primarily responsible for employee development, is a staff department such as HR responsible, or is it the employee?

In the most global sense, the supervisor and employee share the responsibility. However, employee development cannot occur if the employee chooses not to learn, not to develop their skills, nor to improve their performance. It is the employee's responsibility to be willing and ready to learn.

It is the supervisor's responsibility to communicate clearly why, how, and when they expect the employee to improve, and then hold the employee accountable. If the supervisor is going to make these demands, it's only fair that they provide the support and the resources for the employee to meet the expectations.

Different People, Different Needs

Common sense tells us that different employees are going to have different developmental needs. Consider the case of Pat and John.

Pat is 23, fresh out of college, and enthusiastic. He's easily excitable, talks quickly, and is generally thrilled to be working at a computer and drawing a salary. He's also green. Pat, for his abundance of good intentions, can't seem to quit making mistakes on the websites he's creating. He's writing code that isn't functional and is taking a great deal of team resources to troubleshoot. At this (very early) stage in his career, it would be fair to say that though Pat is a poor performer, he is not a bad employee. And so, the supervisor's expectations for Pat would be very different than for John, who is another story altogether.

John is 46 and, never tires of reminding Pat, "was writing code on an Apple IIE when you were still in short pants." That's precisely the problem with John. He's been writing code forever and is tired or bored or something. He's shown himself to be brilliant, but his performance over the past nine months has been lacking its usual luster.

Though both Pat and John are poor performers, their supervisor should behave differently toward each of them. Pat is simply struggling to learn the basic responsibilities of his job. In reality, he's learning from his mistakes and making very good progress on his way to a better level of performance.

The problem with John will be tougher for the supervisor to deal with. John is exceptional in many ways, but John is bored. He is the sort of employee who thrives on challenge and by now, he could write this code in his sleep. Unfortunately, he has another 20 years before he can start collecting Social Security, so it seems both John and his supervisor have a problem to sort out.

The supervisor has two choices here: either expand the job to make it more interesting or work with John on his career development, because he is ready to move on.

The company will lose a valuable resource if John decides to leave. Often this occurs because a performance problem is not recognized for what it is—a problem in development. John, who is an informal leader among the workgroup and respected for his expertise, might drift into conflict with the supervisor. If the supervisor is wise, he/she will recognize the source of the performance problem and work with John to find a win/win solution to the problem.

Stages of Employee Performance Growth

Figure 5.1 shows a typical development curve for a newly hired employee—Pat, in this case. If Pat is typical (and he is) he will go through four stages of employee performance growth shown by performance rising higher over time. Pat's overall contribution to team results is growing.

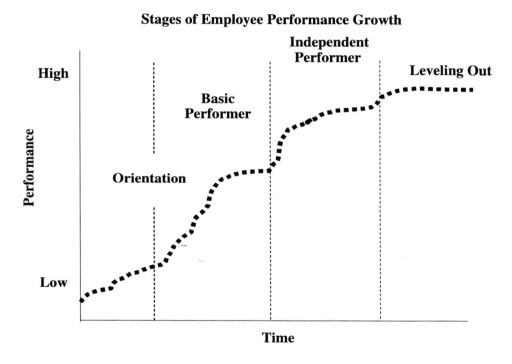

Figure 5.1

Orientation

During orientation, Pat will develop his first impressions about the position and the organization. His performance is not judged very critically at this stage, and his supervisor and fellow employees make every attempt to instill in Pat a proper attitude and perspective about the job, the company, and his co-workers. This stage doesn't last long.

Basic Performance

Pat is struggling to learn the basics of the job, to perform adequately, and to solve problems as time goes on. He has entered stage two—basic performance. Pat is tired and having trouble sleeping as he tries to understand his work responsibilities and how he should get them done. He's become inse-cure about his job and doubts his ability to do what's asked of him.

Pat's supervisor has seen this stage before. He helps Pat along with basic training, and tells him that it will be fine, saying, "Even John went through these ten years ago." Pat is reassured, works through the problems, and moves to the next stage.

Independent Performer

Pat has become confident in his ability to solve problems, handle the job ef-fectively, and make innovations and improvements in the job. He is on fire, receiving frequent high fives in the hallway. New employees ask him how he writes such elegant code.

Pat is motivated and performing independently. His supervisor wishes he could clone him ten times or so and just fill his whole workgroup with Pats. Pat loves coming to work and even occasionally stays late, off the clock, to fin-ish a project. Taking cues from the situation with John, the supervisor starts enlarging the job so Pat won't get the "John Syndrome."

Leveling Out

One day Pat arrives at work and realizes the job is no longer fun. He's not on fire—there's nothing left to burn, just dull code he's seen a hundred times before. He has time left over at the end of the day, which he uses to play soli-taire. He's bored. His performance is high, but he is leveling out relative to his capabilities.

This stage can last a long time and ultimately can cause big problems for Pat and his supervisor. If Pat's frustration builds because the tasks are tedious, he will look elsewhere for a new challenge.

If the situation is healthy, Pat and his supervisor will work together to help Pat fulfill his career expectations either within the work team, elsewhere with-in the company or, perhaps, even outside the organization.

How long it takes an employee to move through these four stages will vary from job to job. For basic jobs with repetitive, routine tasks, an employee may move through the stages in a matter of weeks. For complex jobs, this period can be six to eighteen months, and in higher-level positions, this de-velopment curve can take years.

The same job development stages can work in reverse as well. *The technol-ogy in today's workplace is changing rapidly—an employee can be sitting at their desk as their job changes around them.* This will put them lower on the performance curve until they can learn the new technology. It's as if they were going through an orientation in that new aspect of their job, and their supervisor should handle it accordingly.

As people move through the fourth stage, they then can move on to a new job and start the stages over again. They carve out a career path, or string of jobs, such as shown in Figure 5.2.

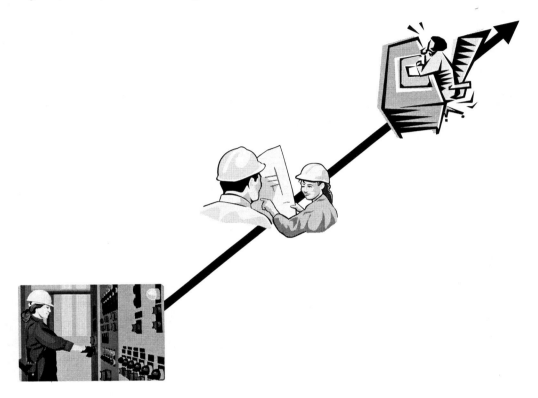

Figure 5.2

Supervisors Style Tips

Supervisors may have employees who are in different stages all at the same time. No matter what stage the employee is in, the supervisor must create a culture of ever-increasing proficiency. For the rookie still in orientation, that may be learning how to use the phones. For a twenty-year veteran of the department, that may be to write innovative, groundbreaking code on a big new project, or help *Sales* put together a must-win proposal. Rewarding and recognizing development helps create the right culture.

Supervisors do this by providing higher standards for all employees, creating a need to learn and the motivation to "stretch" to achieve higher performance levels. If higher levels of performance align with the organization's goals and objectives, the organization itself will grow and develop. Supervisors can do this both through individual efforts with employees and by creating organization-wide expectations for development. Documenting development plans adds weight and urgency.

A supervisor's style or work habits can either encourage or discourage employee growth or development. A workaholic supervisor who prefers to do all the thinking and mission-critical work, likely does their employees a disservice. When supervisors properly "let go" and permit employees to succeed or fail, they create a need for the employee to learn and stretch their abilities. Of course, stage the process and avoid the "sink or swim" method.

An authoritarian supervisory style can condition employees to sit back and wait for orders about what to do which stunts professional growth. Under this style, the employee's motivation to develop will wane.

It is up to the supervisor to provide fitting role models—the old adage of monkey-see-monkey-do might apply here. If the supervisor says that development is important, yet does not show it, the employees will believe their eyes, not their ears. If you ignore employee efforts to show initiative and stretch their abilities, those efforts will disappear.

Managing Development

Supervisors should manage development just as they would anything else, by planning, organizing, controlling, and evaluating. A two-minute discussion of an employee's development plan during the annual performance appraisal does not make a development effort. Successful supervisors know they must invest time communicating with employees about development. In addition, they know that they must monitor and reward progress if improvement is going to matter.

Many supervisors turn to staff departments for help carrying out their plans. Training, HR, and Productivity Improvement departments can be a great help, but the supervisor cannot just delegate the process to them. In fact, centralized departments that take care of all training for the supervisors are actually being counterproductive. Their actions encourage supervisors to say, "Oh, my employee needs training," and simply turn the employee over to the HR or training department to be "fixed." This approach is an abdication of the supervisor's developmental responsibilities. While becoming rare, with this approach, employees likely receive inadequate training and poor on the job follow-up.

When a staff department presents training for your employee, show your support before, during and after. For example, you could appear for a while at the training event or meet afterwards to discuss applying lessons to the job.

The bottom line is to measure training efforts by on-the-job performance improvement. Job performance is clearly a supervisory responsibility.

Development Retains Qualified Workers

When we look beyond the scope of one employee's performance at their particular job, training has a larger importance for the company. The supervisor should be aware that their company might require employee training for strategic reasons.

In the long run, organizations that develop their employees are more socially responsible. Of two companies competing for human resources in the labor market, the one that is perceived to be more developmental in its approach is more likely to succeed. As companies strive to improve productivity by replacing labor with capital investment, automation, and so on, they will see a need to retrain the work force to help them adapt to the new conditions. The future *requires* companies to retrain employees—not to do so is costly.

For example, as companies automate capabilities they have to decide if they are going to lay off employees or retrain them. Every person who leaves an organization takes with them a large amount of knowledge, skill, and experience with the company and its products or services. The knowledge includes intangibles such as company culture, management, policies, practices, and competition. This valuable knowledge is not easily replaced. It is sad when companies have highly skilled people exiting out one door, because their jobs are eliminated or their skills are obsolete. It is plain stupid if it has similarly paid new-hires entering through another door. The organization will have a disproportionate number of employees in the orientation stage and is likely to experience a drop in productivity.

Retraining the production worker to do administrative or data processing work may be less costly than allowing them to leave the company and hiring a new employee who will also require training. As you can see, employee development and organizational health are intertwined.

Bottom line: employee development doesn't just happen. It must be managed and valued by supervisors. Companies see abundant payoffs when they support and reward employee development. The employees do, too.

Training Problem Needs Analysis

Needs analysis seeks to improve performance by identifying the development needs of the organization and the individuals within it. We suggest you call performance problem with training solutions by the euphemism *performance gaps*. Using the term performance gap helps avoid misunderstandings and employee defensiveness as not all performance problems indicate problem employees. Discussing training needs or requirements openly is a great idea, but you don't want to give the wrong impression.

Remember that not all performance problems stem from a skill or knowledge deficiency. Imagine if you are merely trying to plan some training in a staff meeting and start tossing around the words "performance problems." Some good employees could get the wrong idea and start circulating their resumes or scanning the Want Ads! Thus, I suggest the euphemism, *performance gap* for "Can't do" performance problems.

Figure 5.3 shows the gap is the difference between the actual performance and the desired performance. The crucial first step in developing a work team is to identify performance gaps, or problems, and their training causes. *Training needs are the development activities necessary to eliminate a performance gap or problem.*

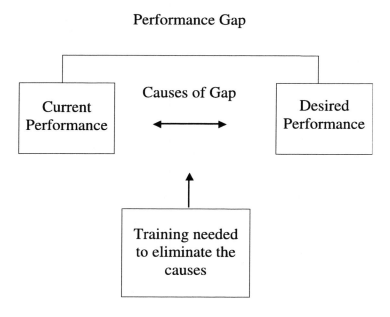

Figure 5.3

A Systematic Approach

When a problem-solving approach such as shown in Figure 5.3 is used, the development and training of employees becomes a systematic way to solve performance problems. Too often, a supervisor decides that a training program is necessary simply because everyone is doing it, or because it is a fad in management literature. This is an inefficient (and costly!) way to approach training. Every year companies sink money into training high-level employees in topics that yield little or no bottom line result.

Two Categories of Training Needs

Performance gaps fall into two categories: Individual employee and strategic. When performing individual needs analysis, the supervisor is concerned with one person's performance gaps. The employee's training needs will vary depending on the stage of performance growth such as orientation, basic performance, independent performer, or leveling out. For example, a newly hired person's training needs would clearly focus on orientation or basic job skills. The supervisor prescribes the training activities and documents them in employee's training plan.

When the supervisor performs a strategic needs analysis, they're concerned about "big picture" organizational gaps, both present and future. Strategic training needs are intended to make sure employees meet organization-wide or anticipated requirements. It is common for these needs to be defined at the higher management levels of a company with input from lower levels. For example, a company requires sexual harassment training for all employees, or a hospital requires CPR training for all. At a department level, an IT manager might anticipate and require all system engineers be trained in advance for a planned hardware or software upgrade. These training activities go into the employee's training plan as well.

If done correctly, both types of analysis result in a set of plans for training individual employees. This two-fold approach ensures that both the individuals' and the company's needs are considered. Write both into an employee's training plan. See Figure 5.4.

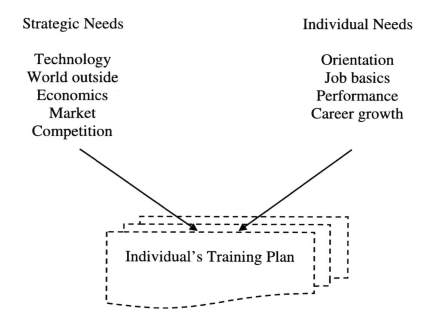

Figure 5.4

Examples of Strategic Needs

The following partial list shows source examples for strategic training needs

- ➤ Quality improvement efforts
- ➤ Cost-reduction goals
- ➤ Upper management strategic plans and mission statements
- ➤ Culture change needs
- ➤ Next year's departmental plans
- ➤ Product/service plans
- ➤ Projected industry trends and technological changes
- ➤ Profit plans, budgets, and schedules

Examples of Individual Needs

The following partial list shows source examples for individual training needs and we will examine this more shortly.

- ➤ Individual performance shortcomings
- ➤ Standard orientation plans

➤ Performance appraisals
➤ Employee career aspirations

So, when does one find time to do all this analysis? Supervisors can incorporate needs analysis into other normal activity. Examples are normal developmental discussions, such as orientation, while doing work planning or project planning, or performance reviews and appraisals. In the normal course of work, the supervisor and the employees identify current or anticipated problems, and discuss learning activities to solve them.

Needs Analysis and Training Plans

To review, the purpose of both the individual employee needs analysis and the strategic needs analysis is to improve performance by identifying the training, development, and learning needs of the organization and the individuals within it. Training needs are defined by performance gaps. Again, a performance gap is simply the difference between current performance and wanted performance as shown in Figure 5.3.

As with any problem analysis, training needs analysis starts with the parties identifying performance gaps, and then discerning their causes. After identifying the gaps, the supervisor, with the employee or team, creates training and development plans to solve the problem.

What approach works best? With professional teams, supervisors commonly delegate most of the planning activity to the employee. They consult, review, and approve the employee's development plan. In other settings, the supervisor may find that it is best to do the plans for the employee, crew, or team. These plans relate directly to the four stages of job growth.

During the orientation stage, the supervisor develops an *orientation plan* for the new employee. During the basic performer stage, the supervisor develops a *job-training plan*, and during the independent performer stage, the supervisor develops *performance enhancement or job enlargement plans*. Finally, during the leveling out stage, the supervisor helps the employee create a *career advancement plan*.

Again, won't this take a lot of time? Maybe not! Consider that the orientation and job training plans may already exist, or once written, have multiple uses. For people in the leveling out phase, your role is mostly consultative. For independent performers, you might assign them to develop their own plans for your review and input.

Once a plan has been prepared, the supervisor and employee agree on expectations and commit to performance improvement goals. When the employee accomplishes the goals in the development plan, the company has a record of performance improvement.

The process is straightforward.

- ➤ Identify the gaps
- ➤ Separate out parts that are relevant for individual employees or groups
- ➤ Plan to eliminate the gap by training and development
- ➤ Document in the employee's development plan

Supervisors, who embrace a developmental prospective, will routinely assess the skills of employees, identify future requirements of the team, and implement programs to meet the requirements. Thus, the supervisor looks at the current skill level, the future skill requirements, and plans training and, or employee selection (hiring), programs to eliminate the gap.

Before looking at individual employee needs analysis, let's look at a brief example of how a supervisor addressed a strategic need, changing technology.

Strategic Example

Tom Johnson was a supervisor of the Circuit Applications Unit of a medium-sized electronics firm. One day, his boss called him in and said, "Tom, the competition is beginning development of a new line of application circuits. In time, our products will become obsolete. We have to get our people up to speed on newer circuit designs."

Tom called his people together and discussed the problem. They had already identified three major skill areas.

- ➤ Familiarity with various discreet circuit components
- ➤ Familiarity with various integrated circuit families
- ➤ Understanding the documentation and block diagrams of the various logic circuits needed for their equipment

Tom knew that precise measurement of individual skill levels would be impossible, given the problem. He chose a team approach to jointly assess each employee's level of competence in the various available and anticipated circuits. He used a subjective, or relative, ranking scale to add some means of tracking progress. Here is how it worked.

He met with each employee. Together, they discussed and ranked the employee's knowledge level on a scale of 1 to 5, where (1) was little knowledge; (2), a casual level of knowledge; (3), a working knowledge; (4), the employee was completely versed, and (5), the employee had used and applied the knowledge.

Tom and each employee discussed and jointly rated the actual current knowledge level, if a current need exists, and if a strategic need exists. Based upon the analysis, they agreed on goals for each employee to upgrade his or her knowledge of the products by various amounts, say from level (1) or (2) to level (3) or (4) over a period of six months. Tom used a handmade form that looked something like Figure 5.5 for Staff Engineer, Pat: While subjective, this approach gave the team a way to discuss and measure progress. It got them moving in the right strategic direction.

Needs Analysis for Pat

Skill	Current Level	Current Need	Strategic Need	Goal
Discrete components	5	5	2	None
Integrated circuits	2	3	3	✔
Logic diagrams	3	3	5	✔

Figure 5.5

Individual Development Needs

Let's reexamine the four stages of job growth. This time we will look from the supervisor's perspective, paying close attention to how individual employee development, or learning, objectives change with each stage of employee growth.

General learning needs relate to the four stages of employee performance growth, which we explain after Figure 5.6.

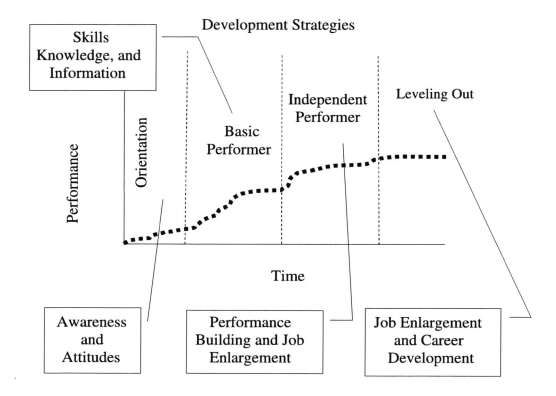

Figure 5.6

Stage 1 – Orientation

The supervisor's primary objective in orientation is to help the employee develop the proper attitude toward the company, supervisor, and their coworkers. Employees need to have proper awareness and attitudes to be successful.

Stage 2 - Basic Performance

The supervisor's objective here is to ensure that the employee develops the necessary skills to meet the basic requirements of the job. Employees need to have proper skills, knowledge, and attitudes to be successful. Remember to focus on the basic requirements in this early stage. "Rome wasn't built in a day," is an old wise saying that comes to mind.

Stage 3 - Independent Performer

The supervisor's objective in this stage is to help the employee develop skills to obtain optimum performance in his/her present job. If necessary, the supervisor will enlarge the job. Employees need to grow and improve to be successful.

Stage 4 - Leveling Out

The supervisor's objective here is to enlarge further the job and to help the employee prepare for a different or more responsible position.

In the next section, we'll examine the training techniques available to a supervisor who facilitates an employee's growth through the stages.

Training Techniques

Training techniques are divided into two categories: formal and on-the-job. Formal training typically occurs in a classroom from community colleges, vocational-technical schools, day and evening college programs, public seminars, internet-based elearning, and company training programs. Vendors also offer free classes to their customer's employees who need training to use vendor products.

On-the-job training is more common than formal training. In fact, experience tells us that nearly all, real employee development occurs on the job. However, formal training is still required as it is more effective in building knowledge in a relatively short time—often this is knowledge that the employee needs to bring them up to speed and prepare them for on-the-job training. So formal training is necessary to build a knowledge base, while on-the-job training helps employees to understand the specifics of what they will be doing.

Formal Training

Most formal training occurs outside the company (at colleges, tech schools, etc.) and many employers reimburse the cost. Outside the more traditional training channels, many excellent resources exist that supervisors and employees can utilize for development.

To get the most out of formal training, meet with the employee after the completion of the training to specify what knowledge or skill they will implement in their job. Write it down. This should be much more than just asking, "How'd that class go?" Be sure to venture into, "Now how can we make use of it?"

On-the Job Training Activities

The following is a partial list of on-the-job training activities:

> ➤ Orientation of new hires
> ➤ Job instruction training
> ➤ Coaching
> ➤ Substitute role
> ➤ Developmental job assignments
> ➤ Job rotation
> ➤ Reading programs

Orientation of New Hires

New hire orientation sessions are typically a hybrid of formal and on-the-job training. These sessions should be geared toward helping the employee develop the right attitude toward the company and the job. To help the employee understand the big picture, the supervisor will stress how the employee's job fits into the total operation, perhaps highlighting the importance of their job performance to other people within the organization. This is a good time to stress any safety aspects of the job. Don't make copies with the top open, for example. Of these, the most important is attitude.

Orientation is a great time to describe and model proper attitude. For example, employees ought to be friendly and positive in his or her dealings with customers, co-workers and vendors. Employees are expected to smile and to possess a smile in their voice while on the phone with customers, co-workers and vendors. They need to be aware that the company has a specific policy about conducting themselves professionally at all times, and are asked to discuss any behavior or performance expectations with the supervisor. All are descriptive examples of how a positive attitude is demonstrated or modeled.

If the employee is being oriented to a piece of equipment, the person doing the orientation will demonstrate the equipment features and help the employee understand its importance to the whole operation. The supervisor should not judge the employee's performance too critically during this stage. Instead, they should focus on orienting the employee with the facilities, the department they will be working in (and the department objectives), and the people. In a successful orientation, the new hire will become familiar with their coworkers and comfortable with their surroundings in the shortest time possible.

Orientation is a crucial process—its success or failure will have long-term ramifications for the employee, supervisor, department, and the company. Ideally, a supervisor handles orientation himself or herself. If they do delegate, it is best to assign it to a person who demonstrates the right attitude as well as task competence. The supervisor stays involved from time to time, and makes sure the employee knows where they can find help. The orientation stage is too important to take lightly.

During this process, the supervisor should take the opportunity to establish a good working relationship with the employee. Get to know them. Tell them you're pulling for them and want them to succeed at their job. Even for jobs that are relatively menial, the supervisor can express the job's importance to the organization and stress the need for pride, completeness, and fairness. Even a person hired as a janitor should have a sense that their job is important, that others will notice their efforts within the company, and that they should take pride in their work.

Have an Orientation Plan

Let's look at some orientation plan examples. Supervisors find it convenient to develop a reusable orientation plan. In Figure 5.7, we see an example of an orientation plan for a company that refurbishes (rebuilds) equipment. The supervisor has identified the various job functions. The team member must know these major knowledge pieces. (You might notice that these are similar to job description areas discussed in the Setting Expectations chapter.).

For each, the supervisor estimates the number of hours to be spent orienting any new employee. Then, they assign responsibility for the orientation to a team member, in this case Pat, who is responsible for conducting the orientation.

For example, a Refurbishment Technician needs to understand the major job tasks on Figure 5.7. The supervisor estimates the time needed to orient the employee to each task and delegates to employee Pat who uses the plan to monitor and control orientation activities. As Pat completes a portion of the orientation plan, he checks or initials it.

Job Tasks and Standards	Estimated Duration in Hours	Assigned Responsible Person	Completed
Understand test equipment	4 hours	Pat	✔
Diagnostic methods	8 hours	Pat	
Component testing	4 hours	Pat	
Acceptance criteria	1 hour	Pat	
Reporting	1 hour	Me	
Other			

Figure 5.7 Orientation Plan for Refurbishment Technician I

Figure 5.8 shows another partial example for a new hire orientation of a maintenance worker.

Job Tasks and Standards	Estimated Duration in Hours	Assigned Responsible Person	Completed
To operate the forklift safely and efficiently	4 to 6 hours	Taught by trained team leader	✔
Proper procedures to use to patch road potholes	4 hours	Taught by supervisor or designated team leader	
Proper procedure to maintain fleet equipment	4 hours	Taught by Equipment Maintenance Supervisor	

Figure 5.8

Figure 5.9 shows another partial example for a new hire orientation for a hospital radiology worker.

Job Tasks and Standards	Estimated Duration in Hours	Assigned Responsible Person	Completed
New Employee Orientation	12 hours	Human Resources	✓
Computer Access	2-4 hours	MIS	
Radiology Computer Functions (e-mail, leave request, register & case edit cases)	4 hours	Supervisor & MIS	
Equipment Orientation and Training (x-ray, patient lift, dry view imager)	6 hours (spread over several days)	Supervisor	

Figure 5.9

Job Instruction Training

Job instruction training teaches a person how to do a specific task and consists of the following steps:

1. Prepare for the training. Find the setting and materials, and think through a logical sequence of how you will present the training. Do not skip this step even if you understand the task very well. Remember you are preparing to train another person, not perform the task yourself.

2. Explain the objective of the task. Why is the task performed? Where does it fit in with other tasks? What may happen if it is not done properly?

3. Demonstrate the proper way to do the task. Accompany the demonstration with a running commentary on the reasons for doing it a particular way. Discuss problems that might arise and how to handle them. Do not skip demonstration.

4. Supervise as the employee tries the task. Check their understanding of key steps by asking specific questions: "Why do you turn that dial to the right?" or "What might happen if you do not tighten the wing nut?" Do not skip this step.

5. Follow up with the employee after they've had a chance to practice for a while unsupervised.

The following example illustrates what can happen when shortcuts are taken. Kevin Wilson was a new hire at McGregor Chemical Company. Herb Mason was his supervisor. Near the end of the shift, Herb said, "Kevin, climb up the ladder on the vat over there and tighten the cover down good and tight," then left to complete the Shift Report.

After climbing to the top of the vat, Kevin noticed a large lead nut holding the cover down. He gripped the nut with both hands and tightened it. It seemed all right, but he wondered. Herb had said to make it "good and tight."

Just to be sure, Kevin climbed down and went to the tool crib for a large pipe wrench. It was his first day, after all, and he wanted to do things right.

He brought the wrench back up to the top of the vat and tightened the nut as much as he could. Suddenly, he sheared off the soft lead nut, shutting down the operation for three days while a replacement was fabricated and installed.

This costly mistake could have been avoided had Herb followed the simple steps of Job Instruction Training. If he had first demonstrated to Kevin how to perform the task, then supervised during Kevin's first try, he would have saved the company much time and money.

Have a Training Plan

Let's look at examples of how these steps might apply to these training tasks.

Example 1, Job-Instruction-Training (JIT) Steps for using a software package

Task: Registering a patient in the Hospital Radiology computer software package in preparation for an imaging exam.

1. Prepare

Log on to computer terminal and Radiology software package. Have a patient request/order available for review.

2. Orient

Explain the reasons why the patient must be registered in the Radiology software package. This task brings the patient information into the software and causes the information to appear on a work list. Also allows images to be connected to final report via computer.

3. Logical Sequence

Patient arrives, Logon to computer, enter Radiology package, go to "register patient," type in patient name, choose correct patient, and go through computer steps to reach statement "patient registered."

4. Demonstrate

Perform all steps to register patient while employee watches the procedure. Be sure to pause for questions, point out reasons and importance of all steps.

5. Supervise

Watch the employee while they perform the steps several times. Provide encouragement and make suggestions, if necessary.

6. Follow-up

Follow up with the employee after they perform the task a number of times. Ask if they have any questions, concerns, or if they would like further training. Check for signs that they are not performing the task as instructed. Provide further training, if indicated.

Example 2, Job-Instruction-Training (JIT) steps to train an employee to forward phone calls.

1. *Prepare*

Locate an office that has a phone to practice on. Explain why the phone must be forwarded every night.

2. *Orient*

Familiarize the employee with the functions of the phone. Explain that the phone needs to be forwarded so calls are not missed after employee leaves the main area.

3. *Present a logical sequence for the task*

Help employee become familiar with the training manual and the section on forwarding phones. Introduce the quick reference guide that is used to continue to learn the procedure.

4. *Demonstrate*

Show the employee what keys to press to complete the task. If the incorrect keys are pressed, explain procedure to follow to fix the problem.

5. *Supervise as the trainee performs*

Ask them to explain each key function and what happens if pressed incorrectly. Ask them how they will remember to forward the phones at the end of each shift.

6. *Follow-up*

Ask the employee to read the manual over until they understand the procedure and practice on the phone for an hour. Return to the employee and ask them to run through the process as if it was the end of the shift. Offer any suggestions on how to perform better.

To be as effective as possible at job instruction training, the supervisor or instructor should understand some basic principles about how people learn.

Tips on How People Learn

People will learn faster, and with better retention, if they receive training that considers the following five factors:

➤ Repetition: The more often someone does something, the easier it becomes. With sufficient practice, even the most complex tasks can become second nature. Supervisors allow time for, and encourage, employees to practice skills at each step.

➤ Timing: People are far more successful at learning if their new skills are used immediately. The greater the time span between learning and application, the less skillfully the learning will be applied.

➤ Variety: Consider using a variety of different mediums for getting the message across including discussion, diagrams, videos, readings, lectures, and asking questions. Switching formats every so often keeps a learner engaged and interested.

➤ Association: Start by engaging the learner on common ground, perhaps using metaphors or illustrations from common experiences, related work tasks, or every day events. Then you can move from the known to the unknown, from the familiar to the unfamiliar.

➤ Positive Reinforcement: Recognize successful efforts by using such phrases as, "You did that exactly right," "That is much better than last time!" or "You are really catching on!" People like to hear good news—it will motivate them to try harder.

Informal Coaching

Many words have multiple meanings and coaching is one of them. In some organizations, the word "coaching" refers to all employee development efforts, but not here. Here coaching is just an informal mode of communication geared toward enhancing performance.

As a coach, the supervisor observes the employee's performance, gives them appropriate feedback, and then suggests ways they might do their job better. The supervisor might choose to "talk through" a logical sequence for performing the work, stressing steps that the employee might correct. The supervisor might demonstrate a task then watch the employee perform it or simply give tips.

Supervisors should be sensitive to the interpersonal dynamics with the employee as they are coaching. Not everyone likes unsolicited advice, so the supervisor might ask the employee if he or she minds some suggestions.

Formal Coaching

A supervisor can use different types of coaching with an employee. Informal coaching, discussed above, occurs whenever necessary; and is a constructive activity aimed at helping an employee with a specific area of performance. Formal coaching is an activity that is usually reserved for professional-level employees and can occur monthly or quarterly.

Essentially, a formal coaching session functions much like a mini performance appraisal. There is an important distinction, however: a formal coaching session is purely developmental in nature and not meant as an evaluation *per se*. One maintains a problem-solving climate throughout the session. It should be a high trust, low fear discussion at all times.

Formal coaching sessions have fairly standard steps:

➤ Review previously stated performance expectations
➤ Evaluate the progress since last meeting
➤ Identify any current problems they're having
➤ List priorities to achieve before the next meeting

An easy way to remember this is to recall the three Ps: Progress, Problems, and Priorities. Record the results of a formal coaching session on a simple half-page document—by accumulating these over the year, you will set yourself up with some nice examples when the time for the performance appraisal comes around.

Substitute Roles

Role substitution takes place when the supervisor assigns an employee to fill in for them in performing some or all of the supervisor's job responsibilities. This technique is particularly useful for independent performers or employees who are "leveling out." A supervisor might choose to employ this technique when they are unable to perform their duties due to vacation, a short-term disability leave, a conference, or a special assignment. This allows the employee to become acquainted with aspects of the supervisor's job without having to assume full responsibility.

Even though the supervisor is not physically on site, they are still responsible for what goes on during this period. They should thoroughly brief the employee beforehand and follow up with them afterward to handle any problems that might have occurred and maximize the learning benefits to the employee.

Developmental Job Assignments

Developmental job assignments are special assignments given to an employee to stretch their abilities and to enlarge their job. It is delegation with a side purpose of learning. For example, a supervisor may choose to have a key employee perform certain troubleshooting tasks to solve specific problems the work team is having. Or, the supervisor may ask the employee to complete a supervisory task, such as the budgets, in order to free up the supervisor's time and to give a potentially promotable employee a new capability they will soon need.

Job Rotation

Job rotation—moving an employee from one job to another—can be extremely formal or relatively informal within an organization. Some organizations have formal plans to rotate newly hired employees in certain job classifications to various departments or work teams for a period—say six months to one year—until they have broad experience with three or four areas of the company.

Job rotation develops an employee's ability to understand special problems and requirements of the organization or team. It also enables the employee and the organization to better assess more permanent job assignments for the employee after the rotation is completed.

On a more informal basis, a supervisor may choose to rotate employees through various job assignments within a team. Such cross training develops empathy for others and makes a team flexible enough to fill a gap when an employee is out.

Reading Programs

Reading programs are perhaps the most cost-effective developmental activity a supervisor can arrange for employees. Larger companies encourage this by funding company libraries. Reading programs make it easy for technical, managerial, and other professional employees to stay current in the various professional and technical journals, an activity that would be too costly or too inconvenient to do as an individual.

Supervisors can encourage employees to engage in professional reading development by assigning them, as a job duty, to review certain current materials and report to the rest of the work team once a month on the contents of an interesting article or book they have read.

Review Questions

1. As an employee, what treatment would you expect from your supervisor who supervises from a developmental perspective?

2. In addition to training and development, what other actions might a supervisor consider to improve work group performance?

3. Briefly outline typical employee development responsibilities for each of the following: Staff departments (such as Human Resources), the supervisor, and the employee.

4. What does strategic needs analysis contribute to the success of an organization or company?

5. What is the purpose of an individual needs analysis?

6. What are the four stages of employee performance growth within a job? For each stage, state the general employee development objective.

7. List five on-the-job training activities.

Chapter Five Learning Activities

1. Orientation

Primary objective of orientation to a job is to set a positive attitude. Select a job with which you are familiar either as a manager, co-worker, or customer. Describe aspects of the attitude you want the employee to demonstrate.

2. Develop an Orientation Master Plan

Start an Orientation Master Plan for a real job, or set of tasks, with which you are familiar. Create at least three tasks and standards, and then complete the other two columns.

Job Tasks and Standards	Estimated Duration in Hours	Assigned Responsible Person	Completed

Figure 5.10, Blank Orientation plan

3. Job-Instruction-Training (JIT) Steps

Exercise: Describe the steps for Job-Instruction-Training for a simple task. You may choose a task for the job from the previous orientation plan exercise. Optional: With another person, act out, or role play, these steps.

1. Prepare

2. Orient

3. Present a logical sequence for the task

4. Demonstrate

5. Supervise as the trainee performs

6. Follow-up

4. Informal Coaching

Exercise: Describe an informal coaching communication for a simple task on your job or outside of work. Optional: With another person, do a mini-role play of the communication.

1. Observe performance

2. Give descriptive feedback

3. Make a suggestion

5. Development Checklist

Check off which development techniques your organization now uses and which you might want to implement in the future. Optional discussion: Discuss the value of the development activities you use now and ones you might use in the future.

Formal training _____ Now _____ Future

Coaching _____ Now _____ Future

Substitute role _____ Now _____ Future

Developmental job assignments _____ Now _____ Future

Job rotation _____ Now _____ Future

New hire orientation _____ Now _____ Future

Job instruction training _____ Now _____ Future

Reading programs _____ Now _____ Future

Counseling _____ Now _____ Future

Positive Discipline _____ Now _____ Future

6. Here is a list of items a supervisor can discuss or do to facilitate an employee's career planning. For each, briefly state how discussing the item might help an employee.

    a. Varied work assignments and developmental job assignments

    b. Regular accurate feedback

    c. Your awareness of development opportunities

    d. Your knowledge of organizational plans

e. Your opinion of individual aspirations

f. Your knowledge of available career paths or normal job progressions

g. Referral to other knowledgeable individuals and agencies

h. The employee's responsibility for their own career growth and success

Chapter Six

Making Performance Matter: Motivating, Counseling, and Corrective Discipline

Chapter Objectives

When you have finished the reading, you will be able to:

- ➤ Understand the root of motivational problems
- ➤ Understand the seven reasons employees appear to lack motivation
- ➤ Perform a simple behavioral analysis before influencing situations
- ➤ Practice the steps of the employee counseling interview
- ➤ Identify the four factors that enhance a disciplined work environment
- ➤ Understand the steps when taking disciplinary action with an employee
- ➤ Identify the components of a performance improvement plan.

Understanding Motivational Dynamics: The Essentials for Success

In the last chapter, we talked about *can't do* problems, when an employee is willing to do the work but lacks the ability or training. This chapter is devoted to the flip side of the equation: *won't do* problems.

In a *won't do* situation, the employee has the ability, possibly even a proven track record of being able to perform a certain task, but is unwilling to do so. The reason: the employee lacks motivation. Hence, *won't do* problems are essentially motivational problems.

Motivation is the personal choice to invest effort and energy into something for a payoff. This definition holds true in both our professional and personal lives. There are two very important dimensions to this definition of motivation: an inside dimension and an outside dimension.

The inside dimension is that which makes up a person's means and drives; the outside dimension consists of the goals someone sets up to satisfy their needs.

To understand human behavior and motivation fully, we must look at both parts. For many people simple survival is their motivation to work—they are simply trying to meet the basic needs of food, shelter, clothing, and so on. People with these needs structure their goals to meet their needs. They work in order to earn a paycheck, to buy the things they need.

Over the decades, there have been many prestigious academic studies about what actually motivates people. It is fair to say that the word motivation is frequently misused. For instance, you may hear a supervisor say of an employee, "Kim is not motivated." A more useful supervisory view is that Kim might be highly motivated, but her motivational goals do not line up with those of the organization. Kim wants to do nothing—in fact; she is highly motivated to do nothing.

Entire books are devoted to motivation theory. If you are not motivated to spend weeks studying them, most of the theories can be boiled down into seven practical ideas. We can think of them as the seven reasons why people appear unmotivated. In addition, a good "rule of thumb" is as follows: If any two or more are present, motivation is unlikely. Here are the seven reasons.

1. The goal is too distant

2. The payoff is too small

3. The path to the goal is too difficult

4. The goal satisfies no personal need

5. The need can be satisfied by a different goal

6. The person works on lower level needs

7. There is a "need denial"

It seems these seven reasons cover nearly all aspects of performance behavior. If an employee appears unmotivated, analyze the situation to find which of these are present, and then work to eliminate or minimize them.

The goal is too distant

Goals less than thirty days away seemed to be more motivating—the more immediate the goal, the greater the motivating effect it had on an individual. This presents an immediate problem for supervisors in that organizational goals are structured, largely, on an annual basis.

For example, a salesperson may have to make hundreds of calls per year in order to meet sales quota. Numerous studies have found that most of the calls and closed sales are made in the last part of the year. In order to overcome this barrier, organizations structure sales goals on a thirty-day basis by taking the annual goal and dividing it up into 12 parts. The salesperson is then measured on a monthly basis as opposed to an annual basis, thus keeping the motivation with smaller, attainable goals.

The payoff is too small

Many employees would not be motivated if they heard their employer say, "Next year, if you work twice as hard, you may receive as much as a 1% increase in pay." People seem to have a mental scale they use to weigh the effort against the payoff for accomplishment. If the payoff is perceived as too small, the goal will not serve to motivate the employee.

This judgment is relative. Working twice as hard might motivate if it saves the employee's job. They can easily make the connection that 100% of current pay is higher than the 0% of a lost job.

The path to the goal is too difficult

Many people believe that it would be extremely desirable to set a goal to double, triple, or even quadruple their annual income by switching to a profession with much higher pay. There is a reason, however, that they do not follow through with their goals. Usually, it is because the path appears to be too difficult and requires too much effort.

Consider Dave, a very intelligent high school science teacher dreaming of becoming a surgeon. He realizes this career move would likely quadruple his current salary, however, he would have to apply to med schools, possibly move, attend classes fulltime for four years, then go through a low-paying three-year residency with extremely long hours. He and his wife have a two-year-old daughter and Dave realizes he would miss her entire childhood if he went this route as well as uprooting the family and taking on an enormous debt load for his education. Dave stays where he is because the path to the goal is too difficult.

The goal satisfies no personal need

Some managers make a motivation error when they try to motivate employees in a large group by saying something like, "If we all redouble our efforts, we'll increase our market share by 22%." As they listen, percentages of the employees will tune out or start texting cynical comments to each other. It is predictable that some employees see no benefits for them, and thus the executive misjudged that company objectives auto-matically motivate. Unless there is a link between the objectives and the employee's needs and beliefs, organizational goals have no motivational value.

One should not assume that "increasing market share" is automatically a need held by individual employees. If the employees were informed they could receive a large cash bonus for the increased market share and believe the objective is reachable, their motivation would rise. Why? Because the or-ganizational goal was linked to their personal needs. Using communication phrases such as, "…and what that means for you is…," or "…and what that means for us is…," come to mind.

There are employees who readily will make the link between objectives and their needs, but many will not. As an aside, few people become supervi-sors who have not already demonstrated that they make the link. They might even be labeled as a "company person" and assume other employees *should* also identify with the company's success. A better assumption is that many people need help linking needs and goals.

The need can be satisfied by a different goal

Let's look at an example of two administrators within the same company; both have a high need for recognition. One may choose to have this need for recognition met by being named best administrator in the organization. The other could perhaps meet his or her need for recognition by being known as the best solo vocalist in the church choir.

This condition is often the most challenging for supervisors because it is difficult to recognize what goals the individual has set up for themselves to meet their needs.

The person works on lower level needs

The psychologist Abraham Maslow developed a hierarchy of needs that is the standard theoretical tool to this day. He understood that people have a vari-ety of needs starting with the most basic (shelter, food, warmth, clothing, etc.) and moving up through security, to social, to ego, to the total self. The chief insight in this context is that people are at different levels of need and the needs can change day-to-day and situation to situation.

For example, take Sven the angler sitting in his boat in the middle of a large lake doing what he loves: fishing. Sven dreams of the challenge of landing the big trophy fish and imagines his photo on the fireplace mantel holding said fish. He is highly motivated by the higher levels on Maslow's hierarchy. In this case, challenge and pride. To meet the needs, he sets up the goal to catch a large game fish.

It's not Sven's day, however, and a large wave severely rocks his boat and he finds himself overboard in the cold lake water without his life jacket. Sven's motivations have suddenly changed. In a blink he forgets challenge and pride as he struggles to survive. Now, Sven's immediate need is survival. His goals are to breathe, swim, and call for help. Lucky for Sven, today he brought along his buddy, Ole, who prides himself in friendship, doing good deeds, and not falling overboard. Thanks to Ole, Sven survives.

It is easy to see how Sven's needs and goals changed with his change in situation. Such changes can happen at work, too. If a supervisor is appealing to someone's pride in their work while the employee is worrying if they will be laid off tomorrow, the appeal to pride may not motivate as much as words that appeal to job security. Where the employee sees their employer as a stable place to work, their attention is more on their work rather than on revising a resume and searching for a job.

Need denial

People can deny that they have needs because they are fearful of change. This is often the case for workers asked to participate in planning and goal setting by the supervisors. Often, the employees choose to deny that they have any need to participate, saying, "That's the supervisor's problem," or "That's the boss's job to solve."

An employee may be very comfortable letting the success or failure of an operation lie solely with the supervisor. It is easier to let the supervisor do all the planning and take on the responsibility, thereby avoiding feeling affected or responsible if the program fails.

To recap: motivation is a personal choice to invest effort and energy into something for payoff. It has two dimensions: an inside dimension that relates to the needs and drives within the individual person; and an outside dimension, which are the goals the person sets up to satisfy the need.

The Outside Dimension

The outside dimension is primarily concerned with goals and behaviors. Since no one can see the inside dimension of motivation, the outside dimension— the employee's behaviors—are all we have to go on. We can observe behavior, but we cannot observe intangibles like attitudes or Maslow's needs—we can only infer them from behavior.

To understand behavior, and how you might go about changing it, it is first important to understand the behavioral model. The behavioral model is concerned only with the outside dimension of motivation. The three pieces of this behavioral model are:

1. Antecedent

2. Behavior

3. Consequences

An antecedent is anything that triggers a behavior, while a behavior is anything that people say or do. Consequences are effects that a person experiences following a behavior.

Antecedents

We all experience antecedents every day. A stop sign might stimulate you to stop your car at an intersection. A telemarketer might cause you to lose your temper. A chill wind might cause you to put on a jacket before going outside.

A supervisor will provide employees with many antecedents in the course of working together. Perhaps a supervisor gives a new employee a particular set of instructions—that may be an antecedent to doing a job as expected. Antecedents can play a vital role in shaping behavior. Put simply, if a person does not have a particular goal, it will not stimulate behavior toward that goal.

Behaviors

Behaviors are what people say or do. The number of deliveries made by a UPS driver would be one behavior. Another would be the number of patient care plans written by a nurse. That Marvin is always late to meetings is one of his signature behaviors.

It is important to distinguish here between behaviors and traits. Behaviors are observable and, to a degree, measurable. Traits are things like initiative, cooperation, enthusiasm, and attitude. You cannot see a poor attitude, enthusiasm, cooperation, or initiative. What a supervisor *can* see are various behaviors that might lead them to reasonably conclude an employee has a good attitude, is enthusiastic, is cooperative, or shows initiative.

Consequences

Consequences are the effects a person experiences following a behavior, such as praise for a job well done, or a high mark on a performance review. Such positive consequences are very powerful in controlling performance. A letter of recommendation, peer respect, pay raises are some of the most fundamental reasons people work. When someone experiences positive consequences, the behavior is reinforced or strengthened.

Consider employees who face criticism, are written up on the job, or have their performance ignored. These are negative consequences, and most people will want to modify the behavior that brought the negative consequence. Negative consequences can be another tool to affect performance, but they should be used only when necessary. Overuse can create a pessimistic climate in the workplace.

Behavioral Model Supervisory Guidelines

There are three supervisory guidelines essential to applying the behavioral model:

1. Behaviors that are followed by positive consequences or rewards tend to be repeated

2. Behaviors followed by neutral or negative consequences tend to be not repeated

3. Antecedents and consequences can be controlled by, or influenced by, the supervisor to see proper employee performance

Here are some examples:

1. The supervisor schedules a staff meeting at 9:00 am—this is the antecedent. Everyone is on time to the meeting (behavior) and the supervisor compliments everyone on their punctuality (consequence). The effect? People are more likely to be on time at subsequent meetings.

2. The supervisor schedules a staff meeting at 9:00 am (antecedent). All the staffers are on time to the meeting (behavior) and the supervisor ignores the timeliness and starts the meeting (consequence). The effect? Remember that ignored behaviors tend to go away over time, so the probability that people will be on time for future staff meetings has just been reduced.

3. The supervisor schedules a staff meeting at 9:00 am (antecedent). Half of the staff is on time and half of the staff is 10 minutes late (behavior). The supervisor takes the 10 minutes to assign all of the difficult and frustrating work to the people that are on time—the easy work was left for the people who came late (consequence). The effect? People who were on time got the difficult work, so the probability they will be on time next time is much lower. Those who straggled in got off easy, so their behavior was positively reinforced. They'll be coming late next time.

Simple Behavioral Model Exercise

Let's work through a very simple example of the Behavioral Model. Here are the antecedent and behavior descriptions:

Antecedent: At a team meeting, the supervisor asks for suggestions for solving a problem the department is having.

Behavior: Alice, an employee, eagerly makes a good suggestion.

Please read the three possible consequences and check whether Alice's behavior is likely to be repeated in subsequent meetings.

1: The supervisor says, "Our management would never allow that."

The probability of Alice repeating the behavior is _____ higher or _____ lower.

2: Right after the meeting, a co-worker snidely accuses Alice of striving for a promotion and refuses to sit with her at coffee break like they usually do.

The probability of Alice repeating the behavior is _____ higher or _____ lower.

3: The supervisor immediately praises Alice, saying, "We'll try to work out the details with upper management, as this could make the department's work easier and more productive."

The probability of Alice repeating the behavior is _____ higher or _____ lower.

Now, let's review the probability of Alice's repeating the behavior for all the possible consequences, and the choices you should have checked.

> For 1, you should have checked "lower."
> For 2, you should have checked "lower."
> For 3, you should have checked "higher."

We can see that Alice's behavior, when followed by positive consequences, tends to lead Alice to repeat the behavior. When followed by negative consequences, the behavior is likely not to get repeated.

Perhaps there is a more important point. What is the difference between numbers one and three and number two?

Possible consequence number one and number three were totally within the supervisor's control. Here, the supervisor had an opportunity to either reward or punish Alice for her behavior.

In possible consequence number two, behaviors of other employees after the meeting could have a negative effect on Alice's motivation.

This points out that there are organizational factors beyond the supervisor's direct control. However, by being aware of them, the supervisor can take steps to anticipate and minimize the negative effects that these consequences could have on employees.

ABC Analysis

A supervisor can use the behavioral model of motivation—antecedents, behaviors, and consequences—to analyze underlying conditions that may create or prolong *won't do* problems. We call this analysis ABC analysis, is merely thinking through the following questions:

> ➤ Does the employee know what performance is expected?
> ➤ Is proper performance rewarded or recognized?

> ➤ Is proper performance ignored?
> ➤ Is proper performance frustrated or punished?

We could phrase the above questions the opposite way to analyze improper performance. For example, "Is improper performance rewarded (ignored, frustrated)?"

Once the supervisor identifies the causes, he or she implements steps to eliminate them and encourage proper performance. The counseling discussion is a practical communication that actualizes the ABC model.

Employee Counseling to Change Behavior

Counseling employees to improve performance is something every supervisor must deal with at one time or another. You will notice that the counseling interview steps reflect the idea of the antecedents, behaviors and consequences in the Behavioral Model.

If a supervisor sees a *won't do* performance problem, they may use the counseling interview to influence performance. "Counseling" here does not refer to psychological counseling, which is an attempt to change some personality dynamic of the individual. "Counseling," as we use it here, is an attempt to bring about performance change through discussion and persuasion.

Before doing employee counseling, examine other factors in the work environment to see if they contribute to the performance problem. At this stage, the supervisor knows there is an important performance gap and that the employee has the skills and abilities to do the job. While thinking about a counseling session, consider the ABC analysis questions:

1. What unsatisfactory behavior is occurring? Note that this question should be answered with specific behaviors. If a supervisor says, "The employee has a bad attitude," that isn't describing a behavior. Remember, behaviors are anything that a person says or does. It is literally impossible to see a bad attitude. However, it is possible to see things that a person says or does reflecting a "bad attitude."

    Attitudes are internal personality dynamics. The difference is more than a semantic one. To communicate credibly about performance problems, talk about the problem behaviors, not on someone's internal personality dynamics.

For example, if one tells an employee, "You have a bad attitude," they can mentally, or verbally, argue about it. In the extreme, they might even think it is a good attitude. Perhaps, they have had it for a long time and become fond of it. However if you say, "The last three times I assigned you to handle the paperwork, you argued about whether or not it's in your job description, even though we already agreed that it was."

2. What behavior is not occurring? This may further clarify the performance problem already identified.

3. Has performance been rewarded or acknowledged? Ignoring it might have sent the message it's not important.

4. Have obstacles been removed? Obstacles such as "red tape," or bad scheduling, poor tools or procedures can frustrate performance.

The Basic Counseling Interview Steps

After analyzing the problem, you might decide it's reasonable to counsel the employee. *When counseling, the two main goals are to improve performance— change a behavior—and give the employee "ownership" of the problem.*

These are the six steps to conducting an employee counseling interview with examples:

1. Describe the performance problem in detail. Be specific. "John, last week I noticed that you arrived to work late twice, once on Tuesday and once on Wednesday. This is becoming a performance problem."

2. State the effect. "Because of your lateness, we now have a production backlog."

    You will notice that steps 1 and 2 are just descriptive feedback.

3. Ask, "How would you correct this problem?"

4. After you've given them a chance to answer, follow up with, "John, how can I help you?"

Be certain that step four does not come before step three. You want them to accept responsibility for change before you offer help.

5. Outline the consequences if the problem is not corrected. "John, I'm glad you'll do those things, because if the problem continued I would have to enter a written warning."

6. Set a follow up date to the review the process. "John, let's talk about this next Friday and see if we still have a problem."

Follow-up emphasizes you will monitor change and demonstrates importance. The follow-up meeting is an opportunity for a fresh start and putting the problem behind you.

The entire counseling interview is typically very brief and held in private. If the problem becomes chronic, disciplinary action usually follows.

Creating and Maintaining a Disciplined Environment

The word "discipline" describes not only a supervisory activity but also a type of work environment. Some work units seem to exist in a state of chaos and confusion and to have many performance problems. Others seem to operate very smoothly. They accomplish much with a minimum of tension and friction. The latter type has a disciplined environment where one likely sees conditions like the following:

➤ Things get done on time
➤ Team members share a concern for quality
➤ Employees have their energies directed toward the job
➤ Problems are solved easily
➤ Punishment is usually unnecessary
➤ Teamwork is important
➤ A feeling of mutual respect and trust exists between manager and employees
➤ The supervisor recognizes that employees' work styles differ
➤ Employees help and train one another
➤ Performance feedback is timely and specific

Such an environment does not just happen; it is created. The supervisor achieves success in two ways: 1) by managing individual people well and 2) by creating an organizational climate that stimulates people to perform well.

To create and maintain a smooth-running, well-disciplined environment, a supervisor sets standards of behavior, provides predictability, behaves fairly, and responds appropriately. Having a disciplined environment helps reduce the need for individual employee disciplinary action, which we address later.

Each of these components is vitally important, so let's look at them individually.

Set Standards of Behavior

Employees expect managers to provide them with clear expectations. They also expect that their work assignments should be reasonable and fair compared to those of other employees. To be fair to their employees, supervisors set reasonable, clearly-communicated standards of behavior for the quality and quantity of work performed.

It's also important to cover other areas of behavior like team work, treatment of others, absenteeism, lateness, personal phone calls, and so on. These are all important areas that affect employees and they should know the expectations and boundaries. Employee handbooks, bulletin boards, and group and individual meetings are some of the communications tools available to supervisors.

When setting standards of behavior, the employee gets an understanding of their question, "I know I've done a good job when…."

Provide Predictability

A supervisor provides predictability by letting employees know what will happen if they behave in a particular way and then carrying out those consequences consistently. If a supervisor is inconsistent with his or her responses to an employee, or treats different employees differently for the same action, employees will be very uncertain about what the real standards are. If the standards are different each day—or if the consequences are different each day—the lack of predictability the employees will eventually undermine discipline and cause productivity and morale to decline.

Behave Fairly

Supervisors who set unreasonable standards for day-to-day activities or fail to provide the resources necessary for employees to meet reasonable standards are perceived as arbitrary and unfair. Supervisors who show favoritism will create double standards that will inevitably lead to an "us against the boss" attitude.

Respond Appropriately

When standards are not met, some corrective action must be taken to bring performance back to expectation. If the supervisor develops a reputation for ignoring problems, employees will soon decide that proper performance is not important because "the boss never seems to notice."

It is important to keep discipline in proper perspective, however. On the other end of the pendulum, the supervisor who responds only in a negative, punitive fashion for things done wrong can create an environment where employees are dissatisfied and unhappy and thus, less productive.

When standards are met, the appropriate response is to reward behavior. Many employees complain, "I can do 99 things right in a day and not hear anything about it. But when I screw up, you can be sure I'll hear something." If this is the case, the supervisor has ignored proper performance. Moreover, as we just learned, ignored behaviors tend to go away, even good ones.

When employees know if their performance is on track or not, with no guesswork, they are free to focus their energy and attention on doing the work, not on speculating about how they're doing in their jobs.

What Is Discipline and Disciplinary Action?

We have used the term "disciplined" to describe the smooth-running work environment. "Discipline" may be a confusing word because people think it always means punishment. For example, young children are "disciplined" through spanking; pupils are "disciplined" by writing "I will not talk in class" 100 times; soldiers are "disciplined" by KP duty; employees are "disciplined" by stern lectures from the manager.

However, the term has several meanings that are not negative. Some others are "rules governing behavior," "the controlling of performance," and "the training that encourages self-development and control." *A true disciplined environment is one where the training and the climate make punishment unnecessary.*

If a supervisor really believes that they are paid for what their employees do, that supervisor will set the rules, control for performance, and give the training that encourages employees to be largely self-governing. This supervisor will not have to use punishment to get the work done.

Of course, problems will occur and employees won't behave as expected all of the time. In those times, the supervisor will use disciplinary action to correct the behaviors that cause the problems. All discipline should be ultimately corrective in its intent—disciplinary actions are really an opportunity to train and mold.

The effectiveness of a supervisor's disciplinary activities should be measured by how much they teach, not by how they punish. They should create, not destroy, morale.

Case Study: Paid Suspensions

Sometimes a supervisor must take disciplinary action with an individual employee. *Discipline is the training and climate that make punishment unnecessary.* Disciplinary action almost always comes after feedback, counseling, and other steps have failed to influence proper performance. The motives are to correct, not punish; and to create, not destroy, workgroup morale.

Here is a case that demonstrates common disciplinary action steps. This company had these, commonly used, disciplinary process steps. (In fact, these discipline steps are so standard as to be almost universal. Remember them for your career as a supervisor.)

1. Verbal warning

2. Written warning

3. Suspension

4. Termination

The company operated under a "12 month rule," which means that if the same problem occurs again within a 12-month period, the employee would move to the next step in the process. So, if they are at step three (suspension) and the same infraction occurs, they would move to step four (termination).

Under their policy, an employee that reached step three was suspended from work for three days <u>without pay</u>. Each time this occurred, the company met strong resistance from the union, thus tying up supervisors for many hours dealing with costly grievances because of the policy.

The company examined the purpose of its disciplinary action and took radical action, opting to give the employee <u>time off with pay</u>. This move emphasized the company's desire to make a disciplinary action constructive rather than punitive.

The employee was able to sit at home, with pay, and ponder what it would be like to sit at home (perhaps permanently) without pay. This possibility was more than just theoretical, as the next violation would lead to termination.

By taking this step, the company eliminated the costly union grievances—as the employees were paid for their time, the union had no issue with the action. In addition, co-workers were less likely to listen to the offender's gripes about the suspension, because they saw it as a "paid vacation." Surprisingly, morale in this regard improved.

This only works well if the next step after paid suspension is certain termination. "The rule" must cover a sufficiently long time, for example, 12-24 months. Shorter "rules," such as 90 days, are easy to abuse.

Performance Improvement Plan Illustration

The performance improvement plan is a written performance warning used for serious performance issues. This may or may not be part of the formal discipline process. The performance issues addressed may be a mix of *can't do* and *won't do* problems. Views on performance improvement plans range from a form of disciplinary action to a get-well plan. This action is often used for some salaried employees instead of the four-step procedure.

Your motivation as a supervisor is to create a realistic plan to help the employee succeed. Before you present this to the employee, be sure you have the support of your manager in the form of a signature at the bottom of the document. In your specific company, there may also be other signature requirements.

Here are some things that go into a performance improvement plan:

> ➤ Problem description
> ➤ Situational context
> ➤ The consequences of the event
> ➤ Your analysis and evaluation of the event
> ➤ Plan and timing
> ➤ Consequences for employee
> ➤ Help available

As you read the Performance Improvement Plan, notice how it illustrates each of the seven points.

Performance Improvement Plan: Management Example

MEMO
To: Al Green
From: Joe Black
Date: July 1, 20xx

Subject: Performance Improvement Plan

The purpose of this performance improvement plan is for you to improve on your performance as Design Department Manager.

1. As you know, we discussed your performance on Monday, May 15th and Friday, June 15th. As we discussed, your workgroup is not functioning effectively. Your project was to be completed by May 1st, and then you indicated it would definitely be completed by June 1st. However, your project is still uncompleted and your revised date is now August 1st.

2. You have also been late on other important projects. For example, you were late by 90 days on the modular chair project and more than 6 months on the china closet project.

3. As a result of your being late, the company has over ten frustrated customers who threaten to cancel orders or go to competitors.

4. Based on my observations, you do not schedule work effectively and have employees standing around because their work has not been properly scheduled.

5. Therefore, I am initiating a performance improvement plan.

   To perform satisfactorily you must achieve the August 1st date for your current project. Your next project will be monitored closely and you will be required to achieve milestones. The plan extends for six months from today, and your performance against schedule will be reviewed on a weekly basis.

6. Failure to correct the areas of unacceptable performance outlined in this memorandum may result in disciplinary action up to and including termination.

7. A Human Resources Representative is available to you for any additional assistance, clarification, or counseling you may think necessary.

_____   _____
Employee   Second Level Manager

_____   _____
Manager   Human Resources Manager

Review Questions

1. Define motivation.

2. From an academic point of view, why is the statement, "Kim is not motivated," a misuse of the word motivated?

3. How might you use the "seven reasons why people appear unmotivated" to analyze a motivation problem situation?

4. What are the three supervisory guidelines essential to applying the behavioral model?

5. A supervisor notices that Hector's friendliness with customers at the front desk has declined dramatically the previous few weeks. Considering the ABC, or Behavioral Model, list at least three questions the supervisor could think about to analyze why Hector's performance might be declining.

6. Define discipline.

7. What four components are present in a disciplined work environment?

8. What should be the supervisory motives when conducting effective disciplinary action?

Chapter Six Learning Activities

1. Counseling Exercise

Below is a brief description of a performance problem encountered by Rita Hernandez in supervising Ted Brown. Read the case for background information, and then look at Rita's counseling statements. Number Rita's counseling statements to put them in the right order. For example, place a number one next to the statement representing counseling step 1, a number two next to the statement representing counseling step 2, and so on.

Background Information

Rita Hernandez noticed that Ted Brown has been absent five times this month. The very questionable absences occur either on a Monday or on a Friday, once on both. Rita feels that Ted is developing a pattern of taking long weekends. Whatever the reason, the absences are highly disruptive. They cause long lines of customers for the other employees especially on Monday mornings when she cannot schedule substitutes. Rita asked Ted into her office to discuss the performance problem.

Number Rita's counseling statements to put them in the right order, starting with 1 and ending with 6.

____   Rita asks what she can do to help him resolve the absence problem.

____   Rita says that his absences, particularly on Mondays, cause customers to wait in line too long and places a heavy strain on the other Tellers.

____   Rita asks Ted what actions he intends to take to resolve the performance problem.

____   Rita describes the performance problem to Ted as a serious attendance problem, occurring usually on Fridays and Mondays, once on both, and reviews the dates of the specific absences with him.

____   Rita sets a date for a follow-up meeting to review progress in resolving the problem.

____   Rita outlines the consequences of failing to correct the performance problem by reviewing the attendance policy with Ted.

2. ABC Analysis, Behavioral Model of Motivation Exercise

Recall the behavioral model of motivation—antecedents, behaviors, and consequences—when analyzing *won't do* problems. When applying ABC analysis, ask the following:

- ➤ Does the employee know what performance is expected?
- ➤ Is proper performance rewarded or recognized?
- ➤ Is proper performance ignored?
- ➤ Is proper performance frustrated or punished?

The above questions could also be phrased the opposite way for improper performance. For example, "Is improper performance rewarded (ignored, frustrated)?"

ABC Analysis Exercise

For <u>each</u> of the following, write out an example of a situation from your experience, at work or elsewhere, where ...

Example 1: "Proper performance" was rewarded?

Example 2: "Proper performance" was frustrated or punished?

Example 3: "Proper performance" was ignored?

Group Discussion (optional)

Individually choose one example that you think others will find instructive. Please label it as either rewarded, frustrated, or ignored. Briefly describe the situation and the outcome to others. As a group, discuss ways that some outcomes could have been more effective.

3. Counseling Exercise

Complete or answer the following:

    A. Review the two goals for, and the steps of, the counseling discussion described in this chapter. Then, answer the following question: What might happen if you get step four in front of step three?

    B. Imagine you are the supervisor handling situations using the six steps of the counseling interview. For <u>each of the following</u>, use your imagination to create a properly worded statement of what you'd say for counseling steps one, two, five, and six.

    1)   An employee has been observed drinking alcohol on the job during a break.
    2)   An employee was reported to have sexually harassed another employee.
    3)   An employee has come in late or not at all on three occasions.
    4)   An employee was observed arguing with another employee.
    5)   An employee has been observed not wearing their safety glasses on the shop floor as required by safety rules.

Optional Role Plays

After completing the section above, choose a situation, or situations, and practice the steps by role playing a counseling session with another person. Complete as many as needed to become comfortable with the steps.

4. Creating a Disciplined Environment Exercise

If you hear an employee make the following comments in a workplace, you would know whether or not the manager had:

A. Set standards of behavior
B. Provided predictability
C. Behaved fairly
D. Responded appropriately

For each comment, write the letter from above that tells what the manager has done.

____1. "It's our policy here in the department for coffee breaks to last no longer than 15 minutes."

____2. "Mary did a really efficient job of planning the conference. We all felt good when the boss took time at the staff meeting to give her credit."

____3. "If I'm late again, I'll get a written warning."

____4. "Our production was down last week because the new cutting tools didn't arrive. The boss didn't penalize us since we did our best by sharpening the old ones."

For each comment, write the letter from above that tells what the manager has not done.

____5. "The boss is easier on his old friends."

____6. "I can do a hundred things right and the boss says nothing. But let me make one small error and she gives me a lecture."

____7. "I never know when the boss will enforce the rule on no personal phone calls."

____8. "Take your time. No one cares when you arrive in the morning."

5. Performance Improvement Plan Purpose Matching Exercise

Match the letter of the purpose with the Roman numeral of its example in the sample plan. The last one, VIII, is already filled in as a start.

A. Give the employee resources for feedback and guidance other than yourself (the manager).
B. Provide descriptive feedback describing the problem.
C. State the effects of the behavior problem.
D. State specifically what actions should be taken by the employee to improve their performance.

E. Clearly state the objectives of the performance plan.

F. State the consequences of failure to meet the objectives of the performance plan.

G. Provide descriptive feedback on the cause of the problem.

H. Document that both the employee and the manager have discussed and agreed upon the performance plan by signing the typed document.

Performance Improvement Plan

____I. The purpose of this performance improvement plan for you is to improve on your performance as Design Department Manager.

____II. As you know, I had discussed your performance with you on Monday, May 15th and Friday, June 15th. As we discussed, your operation is not functioning effectively. Your project was to be completed by May 1st. You indicated it would definitely be completed by June 1st. However, your project is still uncompleted and your revised date is now August 1st.

____III. As a result of your being late, the company has over ten customers who are dissatisfied and threatening to cancel orders or go to competitors. You have also been late on other important projects. For example, you were late by 90 days on the modular chair project and more than 6 months on the china closet project.

____IV. Based on my observations, you do not schedule work effectively and have employees standing around because their work has not been properly scheduled.

____V. Therefore, I am initiating a performance improvement plan. The following are the details of the plan.

      1. To perform satisfactorily you must achieve the August 1st date for your current project. Your next project will be monitored closely and you will be required to achieve milestones.

      2. The plan extends for the next six months, from today.

      3. Your performance against schedule will be reviewed on a weekly basis.

____VI. Failure to correct the areas of unacceptable performance outlined in this memorandum may result in disciplinary action up to and including termination.

____VII. A Human Resources Representative is available to you for any additional assistance, clarification, or counseling you may think necessary or appropriate.

<u>H</u> VIII. (Signatures)

Chapter Seven

Integrative Case Studies: Putting all the Pieces Together

Case Study: Arnold's Computer Services Company

Instructions

➤ Read the general background information and techniques to consider, below.
➤ Read and understand each employee's description.
➤ Answer the questions that follow the description of each of the employees.
➤ Complete your own case at the end.
➤ Use any of the content of this course and your own experience to answer the questions.
➤ Clearly label your responses and be concise.

General background information

You are a supervisor at Arnold's Computer Services Company. Your company provides many computer and network services to other companies. You have been there for many years and are familiar with different jobs and the way your company does business. Your company has just added some new technologies to which your employees are just adjusting. You know that your customers always expect quality, on-time delivery of services.

As a supervisor you must keep in mind that hiring new employees is expensive and that it can be difficult to find skilled replacements for people who leave. You're concerned about the employees in the following five case studies—the other employees are performing well. The employees you're responsible for often work with other parts of the company as well as directly with customers.

Techniques to consider

Following are a list of the techniques supervisors use to correct employee performance gaps. Please reference these techniques, and any others you recall from the reading, when filling in your answers.

1. Descriptive (constructive) feedback is used for both *can't do* and *won't do* problems. Positive feedback is useful in supporting good performance.
2. Motivation and ABC Analysis is used for *won't do* or willingness problems.
3. Training and coaching is used for *can't do* problems.
4. Counseling is used for *won't do* problems.

5. Reprimands, performance warnings, and disciplinary action are used mostly for *won't do* problems.
6. Performance Improvement Plans are used, mostly, for serious problems.
7. Career discussions are helpful for people who are leveling out.
8. Your common sense is used all the time.

Employee #1: John

John is a new member of your team who transferred into your department one month ago from another part of the company. He needs to visit customers at their sites and is often out of the building. He had good performance appraisals from other managers before joining your department. In previous assignments, he worked by himself with little need to talk to other team members.

You've observed that John:

➤ Makes few work errors and he is technically highly skilled
➤ Never completes projects by deadline, although they're not "critically late"
➤ Hesitates to make decisions and often comes to you for help
➤ Is often late for important meetings

1. Briefly discuss which stage or stages of employee performance growth apply to John.

2. Properly specify John's performance problems and label them as either *can't do* or *won't do* problems.

3. List steps or techniques, described in this course, you could use to help John improve his performance. Consider work expectations, motivation, formal and on-the-job training techniques, counseling, and other concepts.

4. Outline at least one specific, action example of what you would do.

Employee # 2: Alice

Alice is a Programmer Assistant. She is a hard worker and has been on the job for five months. She likes to work by herself. Because of time pressures, you have not had the time to work much with her. You felt that any problems would go away after she got more time on the job, and you haven't talked to her about them. The following problems have not gone away:

> ➤ Numerous technical errors in the programs she works on.
> ➤ Other teams report that Alice does not keep them informed.
> ➤ Alice doesn't accept instruction well, especially from more se-nior programmers on your team.

1. Briefly discuss which stage or stages of employee performance growth apply to Alice.

2. Properly specify Alice's performance problems and label them as either *can't do* or *won't do* problems.

3. List steps or techniques, described in this course, you could use to help Alice improve her performance. Consider work expectations, motivation, formal and on-the-job training techniques, counseling, and other concepts.

4. From these, outline at least one specific, action example of what you would do

Employee #3: Albert

Albert is a relatively new Engineer. He works hard and was hired new into the company four months ago. He is technically very skilled and has good technical performance.

Recently, however, the Project Leaders of the two project teams on which Albert works have come to you and complained that Albert is not much of a "team player." Here are the specific problems that are hurting team performance:

> ➤ He does not participate in team meetings and often is late to them or "forgets" to come altogether.
> ➤ He does not help others when they obviously need or request help.
> ➤ He speaks so critically and sarcastically to other team members that they avoid him as much as possible.

1. Briefly discuss which stage or stages of employee performance growth apply to Albert.

2. Properly specify Albert's performance problems and label them as either *can't do* or *won't do* problems.

3. List steps or techniques, described in this course, you could use to help Albert improve his performance. Consider work expectations, motivation, formal and on-the-job training techniques, counseling, and other concepts.

4. From these, outline at least one specific, action example of what you would do.

Employee #4: Don

Don is an Information Analyst. He has been with the company for six years and handles many of your most difficult customer situations. His performance is always top-notch, on time, and creative. In addition, he shows leadership ability in the department by making good decisions and helping employees when you are too busy. He is an employee that you often rely on.

There is a problem, however.

> ➤ Don is growing increasingly impatient for more responsibility and higher pay. You know he has promotion potential elsewhere in the company, but not in your department. You would hate to lose Don at this time, yet you fear that he may leave to go to another company.

1. Briefly discuss which stage or stages of employee performance growth apply to Don.

2. How might you handle this situation? There is no need to specify a "perfect" course of action.

Employee #5: Anita

Anita has handled your customer records for six years. She is a good performer, completing most of her work on time. She prefers to have very clear instructions for her work and follows those directions precisely. Her past performance ratings were moderately good. When she must complete reports her written work is pretty good, however when making presentations verbally in front of groups, she lacks confidence and needs plenty of assurance to get through them.

Here's the problem:

> ➤ Anita was passed by for promotion three months ago. She believes she should have been promoted, and has complained to coworkers, but never to you. Her performance has dropped the past three months and now you are getting concerned about it.

1. Briefly discuss which stage or stages of employee performance growth apply to Anita.

2. Properly specify Anita's performance problems and label them as either *can't do* or *won't do* problems.

3. List steps or techniques, described in this course, you could use to help Anita improve her performance. Consider work expectations, motivation, formal and on-the-job training techniques, counseling, and other concepts.

4. From these, outline at least one specific, action example of what you would do.

Your Case

1. Please describe a performance problem that someone you know has. If you are a manager, choose an employee.

2. Briefly describe the stage of employee performance growth that applies.

3. Is the problem a *can't do* or *won't do* problems?

4. What steps or techniques described in this course could you use to help improve the performance. Consider work expectations, motivation, formal and on-the-job training techniques, counseling, and other concepts.

5. From these, outline at least one specific action example of what you would do.

Chapter Eight
Performance Appraisals that Support the Day-to-Day Strategy

Chapter Objectives

When you have finished the reading, you will be able to:

- ➤ Explain how performance appraisal contributes to managing performance
- ➤ State why good documentation is a prerequisite for accurate ratings
- ➤ State the three major objectives for performance appraisal discussion
- ➤ Practice the steps for conducting a performance appraisal discussion
- ➤ Develop a list of Do's and Don'ts when conducting a performance appraisal discussion.

Performance Appraisals Support Team Performance

Performance Appraisals should support and reinforce the aims of your day-to-day strategies. After all, the reason to do a performance evaluation is to reward an employee for doing a good job day-to-day. Your reason for doing performance appraisals should not be to provide "food for files." Performance appraisals also may have other purposes, such as the following:

- ➤ Employee rankings for salary forecasting
- ➤ Profile employees for promotion opportunities
- ➤ Reward improvement
- ➤ Provide marginal employees incentives to improve
- ➤ Development planning
- ➤ Career discussion opportunity
- ➤ Enhance communication between the supervisor and employee
- ➤ Keep the management staff "under control"

In this book, we focus on how the appraisal helps in the performance management process, so let's revisit what we said about performance appraisal in Chapter 1.

In Chapter One, we mentioned that many organizations require performance appraisals be completed, usually annually. Here's the material from Chapter One, so you don't have to look back.

Performance Appraisals can provide much-needed organizational discipline to keep the management staff "under control." If a supervisor knows that they are going to have to appraise the performance of their employees at some future time, then, they must pay closer attention to what their employees do today. In other words, it helps keep employee performance issues "in front" of supervisors.

In the long term, the efforts of all employees are important, and appraisals can provide a stimulus for supervisors to spend time devising ways to help employees perform better. The appraisal session might be a good time to initiate any such plan.

The appraisal process is formal, meaning that it is written down and a part of the employee's permanent record. This formal mechanism gives supervisors some leverage, or influence, to make proper performance matter to employees and lets employees know that there are positive and negative consequences for good and poor behaviors.

When imagined as a timeline, the day-to-day supervisory strategy is done between appraisals and had three steps:

1. Informally setting expectations

2. Monitoring for problems or performance that varies from expectations

3. Working out ways to bring performance up to, or beyond, expectations

Figure 8.1 The Work Planning and Appraisal Process Viewed as a Timeline.

In a day-to-day work setting, you are *not* sitting down to write a performance appraisal form, or hold a formal appraisal discussion, or set next year's objectives. Now we will.

The Performance Appraisal Is an Evaluation

Evaluations can sometimes be scary to give, and to receive. The performance appraisal is an important activity of the fifth management function—evaluating—and whether we like it or not, they are usually required.

There are all kinds of evaluations in life and at work. These can come in the form of tests or simple checkups. The performance appraisal should be more like an annual health checkup than a Driver's License Test or Final Exam in school. If you think of the purposes of a performance appraisal as being similar to those of an annual physical, you're on the right track.

Just as different people get different health evaluations at their annual checkups, different employees get different performance ratings each year. Let's look at three different situations.

For starters, there are people who are healthy and fit, work out for one hour each day after their nine-hour job, and take no prescriptions. They love hearing the doctor tell them how great their health is! They love being a top health performers, in fact; some want the medical OK to train for a 26 mile marathon run.

Second, we have the generally healthy people, who have some problems, but are in good health. They don't mind hearing some bad news, since most of the doctor's health evaluation tells them they have "no big problems." They are in good health and now know where to improve or problems to watch. They are good health performers.

A big problem medical doctors face is that sometimes they encounter very sick people. If a person is admitted via the emergency room, the doctor will not be too worried about the finer health points. The doctor is in triage mode, concerned about the critical few life or death factors: breathing, bleeding, pulse, respiration, emergency treatment, and so on. Some employees need to perform successfully in the job basics, too, before considering the finer points of performance.

Just as doctors might have different goals for checkups, supervisors will have different goals in their performance appraisals. These goals are driven entirely by where the employee is and where they need to go.

Hundreds of newer supervisors have told me in seminars how much they dread doing annual appraisals. A frequent negative comments is that it is a lot of paperwork with little day-to-day payoff. A noted psychiatrist found in his research that there is a stressful internal dynamic caused by a supervisor's values when they are required to *judge* others. This is not surprising. Most supervisors were promoted to the job because they value achievement and excel at helping others get the job done; not because they were a team's judge and jury or their chief critic.

Most employees look forward to their performance appraisal about as much as an upcoming root canal. After all, appraisals are part of the permanent employment record and have the potential to dredge up all kinds of job security and career growth fears, whether those fears are real or imagined. In summary, here we have at least two barriers to effective performance appraisals:

1. Paperwork with no payoff

2. Fears

If doing appraisals is a job requirement, how can supervisors face, and overcome, the barriers?

1. Make the activity worthwhile

2. Acknowledge that fear may be a factor and take action to eliminate or minimize it

Is Fear a Factor?

If you think fear will affect the climate of the appraisal, ask yourself, "Why might an employee be nervous or fearful?" "Why might *I* be nervous?" There are many specific answers, but here are some general suggestions.

1. It's not your job to psychoanalyze the employee's fears, just to be aware that they might be there. Keep in mind people have different life experiences with evaluations, some harsh. You should therefore take the appraisal communication seriously, knowing that it may affect future job performance and relationships.

    Be sure you accurately explain the uses for the appraisal and include the positive motives behind them. That at least can overcome fear of the unknown. Be accurate about your evaluation—if the employee is an unsatisfactory performer, he or she needs to know it. People are entitled to an accurate evaluation. Fear should never get in the way of communicating the facts.

2. Give employees time to plan and prepare for their discussion by asking them for a *self appraisal*. You might even have them complete the same Appraisal Form that you have to use. That way the discussion can be a two-way comparison, not a one-way lecture. Your job is to communicate clearly the purpose of the appraisal and how it is focused on helping them succeed, not finding a way for them to fail. See it as a two-way discussion over coffee, not a criminal sentencing hearing.

3. "No surprises" is the goal. If you did a good job throughout the year with your day-to-day strategy, employees should not be surprised by anything they hear in the appraisal discussion.

There are exceptions to this, however. A common trait of unsatisfactory performers is they believe their performance is exceptional. In fact, many supervisors report that throughout the year they talked to an unsatisfactory performer "until they were blue in the face" about performance deficiencies. The employee never heard the message until it was in black and white on the official appraisal form.

Make It Worthwhile

Get a return on your investment of time. View the appraisal as your opportunity to solve some of *your* problems. For your strong performers, you might delegate some of your work to employees through the use of developmental job assignments or job enlargement. They will like the challenge, and you will save some time. For unsatisfactory performers, you can see it as a force for positive change.

We will now turn our attention to the goals of a performance based appraisal

Know What Results You Want from the Appraisal

Good appraisals always have a major goal that enhances team performance. The purpose will vary depending on your opinion of the overall performance of the employee. This might be a good time to review Chapter Two, "Thinking Ahead to the Performance Appraisal When Setting Expectations."

Rate the Performance as Top, Good, or Unsatisfactory

You will have different goals for the appraisal, and use different steps, depending whether the employee is an unsatisfactory, good, or top performer. If the word "unsatisfactory" seems harsh, a euphemism such as "partially achieving," might be more tactful. Try not to let wording change your opinion and your goals for the discussion.

When following best practices, a manager bases performance ratings on the employee's performance, not on employee traits or characteristics. Not doing so can also set the stage for running afoul of the spirit of U. S. EEO guidelines and practices.

Consider the following three "big picture" categories when you decide the overall performance level:

Work Results

- ➤ Job Responsibilities: Do employees reliably carry out their job duties? Do they complete their work or project plans on-time and in-line with expectations?
- ➤ Additional Assignments: Are they willing or able to take on work peripheral to their main job?
- ➤ Relative Difficulty of Assignments: Are employees willing to handle difficult situations?
- ➤ Individual Performance Standards: Do employees demonstrate high performance expectations about the quality, quantity, customer service, and other aspects of their job?

Teamwork

- ➤ Teamwork Relationship: Do employees contribute to the overall results and positive climate of the team. Do they help others do their jobs well?

Development

- ➤ Development Plan Progress: Are employees getting better at their jobs and increasing their contribution and value to the company?

Why are results, teamwork and development important? If you ask practicing supervisors how they base their ratings, their usual off-the-cuff answer is "work results." But when they think about it more deeply, they say that *their* performance rating is based on how well the employee team performs *as a whole*, not on how each employee individually performs. There is a big difference.

In a similar manner, supervisors are concerned about the future, so they want their teams to be developing their skills, knowledge, and capabilities to meet the competitive challenges of next year and beyond.

Before you hold the Appraisal discussion, fill out the required form and plan each discussion. If your organization uses peer ratings, or 360 feedback plans, gather and consider that input according to directions.

Good Documentation is a Prerequisite for Accurate Ratings

It is important to keep in mind that performance appraisals are just a summation of performance over the appraisal period (usually 12 months). To be accurate, ratings must refer to an employee's real performance over the period, not just their spectacular successes or failures. Good documentation is essential for the supervisor, the employee and the company—without it, ratings can be emotive or based simply on recent performance.

Good documentation includes:

➤ anecdotal records of the peaks and pits of performance throughout the year
➤ the context in which the event occurred
➤ a timely note written shortly after the event
➤ your analysis of the event
➤ whatever you find necessary to help you recall the total performance picture

It can be tempting to try to save time by only keeping records on problem employees—this is a dangerous shortcut. If you keep records on one employee, try to keep records on all. Every employee deserves an accurate rating; and that means every employee merits documentation, even if it is only a small file for each employee with performance notes you made during the year. These anecdotal records are designed to remind you of the representative performance examples. For the purpose of preparing the performance appraisal, they need to only serve as a reminder of the performance plusses and minuses over the appraisal period. Keep records securely.

Because most companies have unique systems for handling documentation, a supervisor should just follow company protocol on the matter. For that reason, we won't get into specifics on documentation in this context.

Mistakes When Rating Employees

Here is a list of common mistakes to avoid when rating employees:

- ➤ The Unforgettable Event: A significant mistake or outstanding contribution can make a long lasting impression. Sometimes these are called critical incidents. Careful documentation will help avoid placing too much emphasis on these incidents.
- ➤ Central Tendency: Rating all employees average by choosing mostly middle ratings. This closes the door to employee growth.
- ➤ Compatibility: Rating people high if they agree with our ideas or we just like their personality; and, conversely, rating people lower who disagree with us or whose personality doesn't match ours.
- ➤ Effect of Past Record: Letting old problems (or good behavior) affect the way the supervisor perceives the employee's recent behavior.
- ➤ Rating Performance on the Basis of Traits: The person who lacks traits we associate with good people or has those we associate with bad people will get a lower rating.
- ➤ Leniency Effects: Rating everyone high. Usually occurs when supervisor doesn't feel comfortable giving negative feedback.
- ➤ Similarity Effect: Favoring those employees most like the supervisor.
- ➤ Self-Comparison: The person who does the job differently than we did it when we were in that position will suffer more than those who do it like we did.

Choose a Performance Discussion Goal

Once you've rated the employee's performance, it's time to turn your attention toward what you hope to accomplish by the discussion. You will have different goals for the discussion based on your general opinion of the employee's level of performance.

1. If you are meeting with an unsatisfactory performer, *your goal is to achieve basic performance for the job.* After the discussion, you want them to be motivated to master the job basics. You do not want to get distracted by job subtleties or future promotional and career matters. Stick to the basics, and leave those other things for later when they are doing well.

2. If you are meeting with a good, solid performer, *your goal is to enhance their performance and recognize their current strengths.*

3. If you are meeting with a top performer, *your goal is to sustain high performance and career growth.*

Depending upon organizational requirements, there may be other things you need to accomplish during the appraisal discussion. They are setting a work plan, setting a development plan, defining career objectives, and having the employee do a self appraisal.

Setting a Work Plan

Many organizations with MBO and other systems require that a work plan be a part of the appraisal discussion.

Setting a Development Plan

Complete a plan for on-the-job and formal training plans for the employee, as required.

Defining Career Objectives

Holding a career discussion can be a very rewarding part of the discussion, especially for good and exceptional performers. A major caveat is to avoid any statement that sounds remotely like a promotion promise, and to make sure that the employee knows that they, and not the employer, are responsible for their own career success.

Have the Employee Do a Self Appraisal

Before you meet for the discussion, have the employee do a self appraisal. This can be as simple as giving the employee the required form to complete and setting the appointment time to discuss your respective ratings. Employers sometimes require this. By doing the self-appraisal, the employee will be more relaxed and prepared for a two-way conversation.

If the employee cannot do a self appraisal prior to your discussion, then start the discussion by helping the employee do a self appraisal using your interviewing and probing skills. Either way you do it, be sure to include a self appraisal in your discussion.

Hold the Discussion and Use the Right Steps

Keep your main goal for the discussion in mind—it will be your compass during the discussion and keep you from being sidetracked from the original purpose.

Choose the right steps. There are three sets of steps to follow during the performance discussion interview. *You will notice that the steps are different depending on your goal, or overall rating of the performance level: outstanding, satisfactory, or unsatisfactory.* If you think the employee is an outstanding performer use the steps for outstanding. If satisfactory or unsatisfactory, choose one of the two sets of steps. Follow these steps in order.

If your employer recommends different steps, use those. Even though the steps may vary, keep the three performance discussion goals in mind.

Be Tactful

Use the discussion as an opportunity to thank the employee for their contribution, or, for the unsatisfactory employee, express confidence in their ability to improve. If they remember anything, you want them to remember that you took the time to express your appreciation.

No one is ego-enhanced by being labeled "average" or "adequate." Your good employees (this will be most of them) don't want to hear that they are just average. Find a substitute word or phrase such as good or satisfactory in every way.

Please take time to review all three sets of appraisal discussion steps. Notice the similarities and the differences among them. If you are new to appraisal discussions, please try to follow the steps closely—they will guide you away from trouble. With a little real world practice, you will become very comfortable with them.

Steps for Reviewing Outstanding or Above Average Performers

Remember that your goal here is to maintain high performance. After the employee does a self-assessment:

1. Congratulate employee on his or her performance. Review the examples that the employee cited and add any high points that you have noted from your anecdotal file.

2. Review with the employee how his or her performance helps you and the organization.

3. Discuss the form that recognition will take in terms of increased responsibility, promotion, additional training.

4. Move into the area of current problems. Key questions to ask: How long has the problem existed? What can be done to solve the problem? Who needs to be involved in the solution? How much time will it require? Create the outline of an action plan.

5. Ask the employee for ideas about how the total work unit might be made more effective. (Notice we are broadening the employee's area of interest and informal responsibility.)

6. Add these items to the action plan outline.

7. Establish specific date for a follow-up meeting.

8. Thank the employee for the high quality of his or her performance.

Steps for Reviewing Satisfactory Performers

Remember that your goal here is to enhance performance. After the employee does a self-assessment:

1. Review with the employee the positive examples that the employee cited. Add additional examples that you may have from your own anecdotal file. Congratulate the employee on the strengths of his or her performance.

2. Explain the importance of such performance to you and to the organization.

3. Move into the area of current problems. Key questions to ask: How long has the problem existed? What can be done to solve the problem? Who needs to be involved in the solution? How much time will it require?

4. Indicate performance "low points" that you have noticed. Cite specific examples. Ask for possible underlying reasons for them.

5. Ask the employee if anything can be done to make the job easier.

6. Actively listen and restate the employee's comments.

7. Create the action plan outline to deal with all of the problems which have surfaced above.

8. Set a specific date for a follow-up meeting.

9. Thank the employee for his or her performance.

Steps for Reviewing Unsatisfactory Performers

Remember that your goal here is to focus on adequate performance in the basics of the job. After the employee does a self-assessment:

1. Review with the employee the positive examples which the employee cited. Question how important these are to the MAIN duties and responsibilities of the position. Ask the employee for examples of performance strengths and accomplishments for each of the MAIN duties and responsibilities.

2. Review with the employee your own examples of less-than-satisfactory performance for these key duties.

3. Ask the employee for suggestions as you go on how to improve performance for each of these key areas and duties.

4. Discuss each item and the corresponding improvement activities in depth. This is critical for improving the performance of the below average employee.

5. Discuss each area where there is a 'block' to achieving performance as expressed by the employee. (Some of this may occur in the earlier steps.) Ask key questions:
   a. How long has the problem existed?
   b. Who needs to be involved in the solution?
   c. What time frames are required?

6. Ask the employee if anything can be done to make the job easier.

7. Actively listen and restate the employee's comments.

8. Create the outline for the action plan to deal with the problems.

9. Set a specific date for follow-up discussions.

10. Express confidence in the employee's ability to improve.

Final Thoughts

Performance reviews are not always the greatest of tools, and at times they can be counterproductive. Following is a list of performance review pitfalls. Read them carefully so you can avoid them when you are on the supervisor's side of the desk.

1. Neither the appraiser nor the employee is adequately prepared

2. The appraisal interview is a "one way" communication

3. Giving performance feedback in an evaluative rather than a descriptive manner

4. Discussing highs and lows in generalities, rather than specifics

5. The appraiser is unskilled in determining and dealing with the actual level of performance

6. The appraiser fails to set specific objectives for the appraisal interview

7. Giving the impression that nobody thinks much of appraisals in our organization

8. Relying too much on "formal" rewards, such as pay and promotions, to provide encouragement

9. Lack of a specific action plan to close the performance gaps

10. Lack of follow-up to ensure that the action plan is implemented

11. The appraiser does not really know what the employee is actually doing

12. The employee feels that her or his performance is superior to that of the person who is conducting the appraisal

Review Questions

1. How does the performance appraisal activity support the aims of the day-to-day performance management strategy?

2. What categories or aspects of performance might you consider when deciding if an employee is a top, good, or unsatisfactory performer?

3. How will good documentation help a supervisor determine an accurate performance level rating?

4. What should a supervisor be cautious about when keeping anecdotal records?

5. What are the benefits of an employee's doing a self appraisal?

Chapter Eight Learning Activities

1.   Performance Appraisal Exercise: Do's and Don'ts

Imagine you are an experienced supervisor who is coaching Jo, a new supervisor. She tells you that she is nervous about giving her first series of employee performance appraisals. So far, she has done a good job setting expectations and correcting performance.

Jo asks you for tips about what to do, and what not to do for effective appraisals. In other words, she seeks lists of "do's and don'ts" List at least two "do's" and two "don'ts." Briefly—in one or two sentences—explain why each is important.

2.   Performance Discussion Goals Discussion

Setting a goal for the performance appraisal discussion is important to getting the results you want. The text suggests that your goals are different depending on your general opinion of the employee's performance level.

Discuss

Using your current or past work experience as a guide, describe how you form your performance opinion of employees, or, as an alternative, of coworkers. Please include general details of your situation.

Appendix, Supervisory Management: A Brief Review of the Bigger Picture

Introduction

Performance management activity fits well with the management process view of management. Here is a quick review of the management process to provide a big picture context for managing performance. *Careful readers will see a secret to ace the quiz at the end.*

Objectives

When you have finished the reading, you should be able:

- ➤ To define management
- ➤ To state the two concerns of management
- ➤ To state the five functions of management
- ➤ To relate management activities to management functions and processes

A Quick View of Management

Management is getting *work* done through (and with) other *people*. Supervisors have a constant *balancing* act: to get the work out while respecting and caring for the people who do the tasks required. If a supervisor can do his or her work without losing sight of either side of this equation, they will be successful.

When managing, the supervisor uses the management process. He or she will:

- ➤ develop plans and analyze work to be done
- ➤ set priorities
- ➤ select workgroups and assign work
- ➤ follow up to see that work is done
- ➤ review completed work
- ➤ anticipate, analyze, and solve problems

Not too bad, right? In their downtime, the supervisor assumes responsibility for their workgroup's contributions and carries out the management process.

The Management Process

Management is essentially a series of five basic functions in a perpetually-repeating *cycle*. When all of the five functions are done, one has completed the management process (also referred to as the management cycle).

The *five* functions of management must be performed in this exact order—if they are done out of order, the process will be unsuccessful.

The Management Process

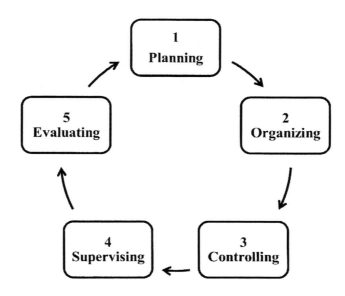

Planning

When *planning*, the supervisor sets the direction with the workgroup, figuring out what they need to do and what resources they will need to do it. *A planner sets an objective that lays out a timeframe and a detailed list of resources the workgroup will need to make the goal.*

Suppose a supervisor says, "I'm going to produce 100 table lamps." That is not a plan. It states an intention, and is perhaps a laudable goal, but there are no specifics. How will you make 100 lamps? When? What will you do with them?

Now suppose that same supervisor says, "I'm going to produce 100 custom table lamps, starting on January 7th and ending on January 14th, at a cost of $5000 dollars. I plan to use 10 people, 400 person hours of labor, 50 pounds of sheet metal, 100 sockets, and 800 feet of wire." Now *that* is a plan.

What's the difference? A plan specifies an objective and details the time and resources needed to get there.

You can always tell when you're listening to a good planner—they give clear mental images of targets, defining things carefully along the way. And, conversely, you can tell when you are not listening to a good planner—this is the guy who walks through the office door Monday morning and says, "Well, what should we do today? Any suggestions?"

Planning is essential before performing the other four management functions. Planning, by its very nature, is oriented toward the future; when planning, the supervisor is attempting to deal with the uncertainties and risks of the future. By starting a production plan for building table lamps, the supervisor can order raw materials months in advance. This reduces the risk of a production delay because materials cannot be purchased and delivered at a later time when they are needed for production.

Supervisory planning actions, then, are essentially methods for managing risk. They are a way for the supervisor to influence the future in a positive way or to react to an unforeseen circumstance.

Suppose a supervisor is ordering materials for an upcoming production run and discovers that a previously-reliable vendor won't be able to have the materials there on time. No sweat: the supervisor calls alternate sources and the materials arrive before work is delayed.

Without planning, a supervisor would be at the mercy of all events and situations as they happen, a victim of the future.

Organizing

OK, you've got your plan. What's next? That would be *organizing: allocating people and resources in the proper sequence*, so that the workgroup can meet the objectives specified by the plan.

Remember those ten employees building the lamps? This is when the supervisor will assign them their tasks. One will fabricate parts, one will prepare wires, sockets and plugs, one will solder, four will assemble, one will paint, one will inspect and test, and one will crate them up for shipping.

Sometimes an organization is good at planning, but still runs into trouble implementing the plan. Usually it is because they haven't established a *sequence* that allocates the resources needed to accomplish the objective. Symptoms of this are departments competing with each other for resources, a seeming shortage of people power, or not enough time and money for the project. This can happen even with a clear and specific plan.

We can see, then, that if the sequence is not correct, organizing can become a source of great conflict within organizations.

Many supervisors find that there are a number of pre-made decisions affecting their organizing process: the lines of authority are set within the corporation, and there are rules on how they can use people and resources.

However, the supervisor *does* have the authority to perform the following three organizing responsibilities:

> ➤ Holding people accountable for their portion of the plan
> ➤ Delegating authority
> ➤ Assigning duties or tasks to be performed

Organizing, then, provides a sequence, allocating resources to meet a planned objective. A wise planner will consider the organizing steps in the planning sequence and save a lot of headaches down the line.

Controlling

Now the lines are rolling. There is a plan, an organized sequence of events: is it actually happening the way it was scripted? Why or why not? If actual work is short of plan, how much is it falling short? Are we making *progress*?

Controlling is the other side of planning—real-time adaptation and course correction. The best plans in the world will fail without adequate controls. When controlling, the supervisor monitors *progress* toward the objectives to see if the work group is on or off target. The essential thing to remember for supervisors is that *good control allows for time to correct.*

Suppose a supervisor hears, "Last month you were $500 over budget." He or she will probably be frustrated. The situation is over and done with and there is nothing they can do about it. This unfortunate declaration is what's known as a historical control. It is too little and too late.

Here's another illustration of controls in action. Suppose an airline pilot is starting out on a flight. He begins with a detailed flight plan; it will tell the pilot exactly how to fly from one city to another. Once the pilot gets into the airplane, closes the cockpit door, starts the engine, speeds down the runway, and enters the air, the plan becomes a useless document unless there are adequate controls. Once in the air, the pilot must rely on all the avionic controls in the aircraft to learn if the plane is flying at the correct altitude, in the correct direction, and at the correct speed.

Without these checkpoints along the way, the pilot would not know if he were flying according to plan. The pilot would not know if they were flying, let's say, from New York to San Francisco or from New York to Los Angeles. Controls are tools and methods that give the plan life and validity as it is implemented.

Controls can, of course, go terribly wrong. Most frequently this takes the form of over controlling (also known as micromanaging). This often bears a striking resemblance to a supervisor with a clipboard making rounds every 15 minutes like a prison guard, tisking and hinting ominously about upcoming performance reviews.

Granted, occasionally an employee will be out of line or not be contributing as they should, and this may require counseling or other corrective steps which are outlined in other chapters.

However this sort of constant peering over someone's shoulder, nagging them to perform differently is never called for. It represents an attempt to control the people, not the plan. People resent controls aimed at their minute-by-minute behaviors instead of their progress toward an objective. This sort of over controlling is overt manipulation, and nobody likes to feel manipulated.

A wise supervisor will focus instead on having control over the plan. As an ancillary benefit, by controlling the plan they simultaneously control the work output of the employees.

Supervising

Let's say you have a specific plan, you are organized and in sequence, and the operation is running. What are you doing next?

You are leading, motivating, coaching, and training those working under you. You are overseeing them in the day-to-day performance of their jobs. You are *supervising*.

The word "supervising" can have some weighty overtones, but it is nothing more than *directing the human effort to implement the plans that have been set.*

Evaluating

Evaluating is comparing actual results to the planned results. Evaluating and controlling are very similar, and some authors lump evaluating with controlling. Here we will consider it to be a separate function of management because the performance appraisal activity of performance management is more of an evaluation than a progress check.

Evaluating will tell you if the plan worked—after all the hard work of planning, organizing, controlling, and supervising, this is the time to find out what went right and what went wrong. Without this step a supervisor would never be able to repeat successes or learn from mistakes.

If the actual results achieved by the team fall short of those called for in the plan, the supervisor will see a performance gap. Say a supervisor planned to build 100 custom lamps in a week but actually only succeeded in building 80—there is a performance gap of 20 lamps.

Taking a hard look at performance gaps is very important in the evaluating process. This is a process that occurs in companies of all sizes, and the same basic evaluating concepts apply for both a mom and pop shop and a Fortune 500 company.

There are three important criteria that the performance gap is examined against:

1. Size of gap—if large enough, the gap can put you out of operation

2. Reasons for the gap

3. The solution to it—this is where follow-up is important

Now doesn't evaluating seem to be a rational and reasonable task for supervisors?

It *is* perfectly rational and reasonable and yet in many organizations it does not occur. In these organizations performance gap analysis is replaced by excuses. A supervisor might hear, "We could have done our part if marketing had given us a correct forecast."

"Well, if purchasing had ordered the materials we needed in advance . . ."

"Well, if engineering had not made an error in the designs . . ."

This is not performance gap analysis. This is the blame game, and it is not helpful. People throughout the organization are passing the buck instead of taking responsibility for their own results.

In some corporations, performance appraisals are a way of checking employees to be certain they are contributing as required and helping them to grow in their job capacities. Knowing that each employee is pulling their weight can be helpful in gap analysis.

If the organization really looks at the size and reasons for gap, next time around they can:

➤ Plan to get the forecast in advance
➤ Have engineering check plans before they're released
➤ Meet with purchasing so they can supply parts on time

When the supervisor engages in gap analysis, he or she may find out that the original objective was not really possible in the first place. If the supervisor discovers this, he or she can then readjust expectations for subsequent projects.

Management Process and Activities Fill-in-the-Blank Quiz

To review and check your understanding, please complete the following quiz by filling in the blanks.

1. Management is getting _____ done through (and with) other _____.

2. Supervisors have two concerns: a concern for the task and a concern for the people who do the task. To be effective these two concerns must be kept in _____.

3. The management process is a _____ that is repeated endlessly.

4. There are _____ processes, or functions, in the management cycle.

5. Fill in the management functions in the order in which they should be performed:

_____ , _____ , _____ , _____ and _____ .

6. When planning, the supervisor sets an objective that specifies a _____ frame and _____ needed to hit the objective.

7. When organizing, the supervisor allocates the resources and people needed in the proper _____ in order to hit the objective.

8. When controlling, the supervisor monitors _____ toward the objectives to see if the work group is on or off target.

9. When supervising, the supervisor _____(s) the human effort to implement the plans that have been set.

10. When evaluating, the supervisor measures actual results and _____ them to planned results.

Bibliography

Institute for Certified Professional Managers. Management Skills I: Foundations of Management. New York: McGraw-Hill Companies, 2006.

Institute for Certified Professional Managers. Management Skills II: Planning and Organizing. New York: McGraw-Hill Companies, 2006.

Institute for Certified Professional Managers. Management Skills III: Leading and Controlling. New York: McGraw-Hill Companies, 2006.

W. Frederick Hawkins. Supervisory Success. Minneapolis: APTI, Inc., 1987, 1983.

W. Frederick Hawkins. The Supervisor as a Trainer. Minneapolis: APTI, Inc., 1983.

Endnotes

i   Just-in-Time (JIT) or Material Requirements Planning (MRP)

ii   For further description, see Management Process in the Appendix

iii   Gibb, J. R., "Defensive Communication." *The Journal of Communication*, 1961, 2|3~, 141-148.

iv   Robert F. Mager and Peter Pipe, *Analyzing Performance Problems: Or, You Really Oughta Wanna--How to Figure out Why People Aren't Doing What They Should Be, and What to do About It.* Center for Effective Performance, 1997)

v   Materials in figure 4.1 are drawn in part from principles in *Analyzing Performance Problems: Or, You Really Oughta Wanna--How to Figure out Why People Aren't Doing What They Should Be, and What to do About It* by Robert F. Mager and Peter Pipe (Center for Effective Performance, 1997)

vi   Most of the time, supervisors use these "won't do" methods in the order they appear.

vii   Management Information System or MIS

Index